KETO MEAL PREP
Cookbook for Beginners

Quick & Easy Prep-and-Go Recipes to
Lose Weight, Stay Healthy and Live Longer

Patricia Young

Warning-Disclaimer

The purpose of this book is to educate and entertain. The author or publisher does not guarantee that anyone following the techniques, suggestions, tInstant Pots, ideas, or strategies will become successful. The author and publisher shall have neither liability or responsibility to anyone with respect to any loss or damage caused, or alleged to be caused, directly or indirectly by the information contained in this book.

Contents

Seafood Recipes 66

Snacks & Side Dishes 72

Introduction

Have you ever had the feeling that your life has become dominated by activities revolving around working and organizing food, and a typical week consists of waking up in the morning, rushing to work, commuting, working, hasty lunch break, commuting home, eating dinner, running errands? Then you may have noticed there's not much time left for anything else. Not to mention the money flowing out of your wallet to satisfy any food whims.

Can't resist buying from a burger stand or dropping into a bakery for a croissant? The world doesn't end if you do so once in a while. However, if added up, you may quickly realize you are spending too much money on stuff you could easily do without.

We may argue that's just the way life is or not, but one thing is for sure - it doesn't take much to make it way better. Planning meals in an organized way for the whole week (or more) may sound like a significant investment but, in reality, it saves us a lot of time and money.

How much happier would your family, partner, or friends then be? How much would you develop yourself, having more time to follow a passion or hobby? How much money would there be left in your pocket if you stopped spending it randomly whenever you have a whim?

If you wonder if a conventional cookbook can offer you so much, the answer is simple - NO. Not a conventional one. But this Keto Diet Meal Prep cookbook – oh YES!

Whether we like it or not, our world is accelerating and new forms or cooking are springing. This book is a culinary response to that acceleration and modern people's needs.

Let's begin.

Keto Diet

Switching to a new diet with the purpose to cleanse your body and burn fat at the same time, can be a tricky process. Most diets require a set of various ingredients, but the ketogenic diet is very specific when it comes to preparing the meals - no carbohydrates, sugars, but lots of fats and proteins. This can prove to be quite tricky for people who aren't prone to spend too much time in the kitchen.

Consuming large amounts of carbohydrates, proteins and fats is nothing to be scared of if you are careful not to eat in excess and you exercise on a regular basis. However, you don't have to be a nutritionist to know that excess of any kind can cause obesity and serious health problems. `Feeding' your body with big amounts of carbohydrates, fats, and protein stimulates the insulin increase, and you become leptin resistant. Moreover, the body weight grows slowly but surely. Uncontrolled diets rich in carbohydrates, fats, and protein can lead to obesity and can increase the risk of heart diseases, cholesterol, high blood pressure, cellular damage and so on.

The ketogenic diet has become extremely popular today, but it is not a new diet at all. In fact, it was created back in the early 1920s by researchers who worked in the Josh Hopkins Medical Center, while they were trying to find a way to decrease the number of seizures in epileptic children. After thorough research, scientists have discovered that food rich in carbohydrates is actually the main reason why epileptic children have frequent seizures. After the epileptic patients were switched to a ketogenic diet consisting of food rich in fats, proteins and only a little amount of carbohydrates, the number of seizures decreased significantly.

SO WHAT EXACTLY HAPPENS WHEN YOU START YOUR KETOGENIC DIET?

This diet's main purpose is to re-shift your body and place the whole 'machinery' on a whole new track. In the Keto diet, the body burns fats much faster than carbohydrates, which is why the meals will be quite rich in fats. The carbohydrates intake is not prohibited, but you will consume them less. Carbohydrates are the body's main fuel or brain's food (our body turns carbs into glucose). Replacing the carbohydrates with fats makes the body find a substitute source of energy to stay alive. The food poor in carbohydrates basically forces the liver to turn all the fats into fatty acids and ketone bodies. The ketone bodies go straight to the brain and take the place of glucose, giving the brain the needed energy and 'fuel'. High level of ketone bodies in the blood will work not only as a great way for your body to burn all the fats, but it will also decrease the possible risks of seizures, diabetes, cholesterol and so on.

Many people wonder why this diet became such a huge hit among healthy people who only want to lose weight, or cut carbs from their diet even if they have absolutely no traces of epilepsy.

Nutritionists are very vocal about this diet, recommending it as a great way of cleansing your body of toxic substances, eliminating risks of fatal illnesses, losing weight and helping stay fit.

Once you start consuming food based on this diet, your body shifts in the state of "ketosis". This is a metabolic state where your body takes energy from the ketone bodies created in your blood and not from the glucose, as before. Your diet is rich in fats and proteins and has significantly lower levels of carbohydrates.

You will notice the differences between the ketogenic state and the glycolytic state; the higher the ketone levels in your blood, the more your body will use the fats to burn and turn them into energy. The results of losing weight with the keto diet are immediate. The excellent thing with this diet is that it will not cause you any weight problems; you will lose all the fat and weight until your body reaches a balanced and healthy fat level. This diet is recommended for life, not only for a couple of weeks until you lose a few kilograms and then return to your old eating habits.

Many people are afraid it will be hard for them to get used to life without carbohydrates, but the truth is you will only need several days of low-carb food intake (about 20 grams per day) before actually witnessing the weight changes. Many people who were sworn they couldn't live a day without bread, potatoes, rice, milk products or noodles, were amazed by the instant weight loss and actually did not want to go back to their old eating habits.

This is a diet that requires spending some time in the kitchen, to prepare your meals. The ketogenic diet does not 'allow' you to eat unhealthy snacks between meals, such as potato chips, cookies or chocolate. If you plan to eat unhealthy snacks between meals, then you are going to fail from the start; not only these will pack your body with sugar and other empty calories, but your body may also get confused about the sudden intake of carbs and sugars. So instead of turning towards the fats as its main fuel, it may start using these ingredients as body energy (therefore the process of losing weight will significantly slow down).

The ketogenic diet increases the ketone levels in your body and you can achieve this process either by strictly following the ketogenic diet recipes or by fasting, although for some people this might be a more challenging start.

Most people think that fasting is starving, but it is not. Your keto diet will work perfectly well even if you don't fast, but in case you do want to try this and increase the levels of ketones in your body, then you need to know how fasting works.

Never try to fast for a long time! Always start your fasting with smaller time-frames and make sure you actually eat. People, who want to increase the ketones in their body and try fasting, always stick to hour ratios such as 19/5. This means that you have five hours time-frame in your day when you can eat your food, while the rest of the time you don't eat at all. It is up to you to set the eating hours (based on your daily habits, working hours, weight, the possibility of enduring without food and so on). If you are new to the ketogenic diet, then you can dedicate one day of the week to fasting. As time goes by and you feel stronger to endure a fasting day you can add more days of the weeks. In case of fasting doesn't work for you, then you do not need to do it.

Consuming meals prepared based on the ketogenic diet will do miracles without fasting as well.

KETO DIET HEALTH BENEFITS

People who switch their diet to the ketogenic diet are not only going to lose weight much easier, but they will also get many benefits along with this way of eating. You will suddenly realize that you are not as hungry as you used to be and this is due to the fact that you are finally consuming good calories and not empty ones that take your entire energy as it usually happens with sugars and carbohydrates.

Whenever you start a new diet, you usually have to face the ugly side effect called hunger; more often than not, diets cause hunger, which surely leads towards breaking the diet. The reason why this happens is that this type of weight loss diets offers less food, instead of cutting the main culprits that slow down the metabolism. Consuming food low in carbs will instantly lead to a lower appetite. You will feel full enough, even though carbohydrates and sugars will be significantly or completely cut down from your diet. When you cut down the carbs, the appetite naturally lowers down, taming your 'urge' to eat chocolate, bread, rice, potatoes or any other food that has carbs or sugars. Your body no longer needs it and it feels full of the food rich in proteins, minerals, vitamins, and fats. The carbs intake should not necessarily be cut off, but you can, in the range of suggested carbohydrate intake based on this diet, consume healthy carbs (but only after you have reached your goal weight).

The ketogenic diet will successfully burn all your fats, making you visibly slimmer. Now your body fats are your main body fuel.

A person's body has subcutaneous fat, which is usually stored below the skin and visceral fat, that is usually found in the abdominal cavity. Visceral fat is the `bad` fat that stores around the organs and consuming it in big amounts can cause insulin resistance, inflammation, and slow metabolism. You don't necessarily have to be overweight to have fat around your organs. This is why this diet is a sure way to cleanse your body, even the parts that are not visible. In general, the ketogenic diet has a great effect when it comes to reducing the abdominal fat that puts you at serious risk of all sorts of diseases, especially type 2 diabetes.

By consuming ketogenic meals, you also lower the level of the triglycerides, as well. These are fat molecules, which put you at risk for heart diseases. The larger the level of triglycerides, the bigger the risk.

The keto diet offers you meals that will help you increase cholesterol that is good for your body. After all, this is a diet rich in fats; the good cholesterol will remove the bad cholesterol leading it straight to the liver, where the liver will excrete it or reuse it. The more good cholesterol you have in your body, the lower the risk of getting clogged blood vessels or heart attacks.

The keto diet is excellent for people who already have diabetes. Consuming carbs in high amounts surely gives the body energy, but most of it will be turned into glucose, which doesn't work very well for people with diabetes. The glucose goes straight into the bloodstream and raises the sugar levels. Your body will create the hormone insulin, which commands the cells to bring the glucose into the cells; this is when the glucose becomes the body fuel (the glucose is burned or restored in the cells). If you are healthy, this isn't much of a problem. However, if you have diabetes, this can become a life threat. If you are insulin resistant, your cells aren't able to detect the insulin, making it hard for the body to bring sugar into the cells. This process is what causes type 2 diabetes. When the body is not capable of secreting insulin to lower the sugar after you consume it, then you will have serious problems with any regular diet that has a significant amount of sugar or carbohydrates. The keto diet will put your body in the state of ketosis, giving your brain ketones as the main fuel.

There will be no sugars or carbohydrates to give you energy, which is why the body will turn towards the next best thing – the fats.

Believe it or not, people who consume ketogenic meals have clearer minds, focus better and feel more energized. It seems that all the energy your body was getting from the glucose was always a poor source (this is why you constantly needed to eat more carbs and sugars to feel full and more energized). Your body can consume much more fats than carbohydrates, so when the fats become the main fuel and are burned at the same time, it seems that they are a never-ending energy source.

WHAT TO EAT?

As mentioned before, the ketogenic diet is a diet rich in fats and proteins and allows just a little percentage of carbohydrates intake. In general, a keto diet contains high amounts of healthy fats (up to 80 percent) including coconut oil, olive oil, palm oil, nuts, and seeds and so on. Fats are the most important part of this diet because they become the main energy fuel. Fats will provide you with energy and will keep you full during the entire day.

If you wonder whether fats will be the only food in this diet, the answer is NO. Keto meals also offer recipes with all types of non-starchy vegetables. You can eat plenty of broccoli, leafy greens, asparagus, cucumber, and zucchini. In fact, you can use these vegetables to prepare all sorts of foods, not only salads (you can make veggie pizza dough, steam them, eat them raw or combine them as a garnish with your main dish).

All foods that are high in protein but have low levels of carbohydrates are recommended in this diet; you can eat fish, organ meats, full-fat dairy products, meat that comes from animals that were fed with grass only and so on. The foods you ought to avoid at all costs are noodles, rice, potatoes, processed foods, foods that contain white flour, desserts and other food rich in empty calories that keep you full only for a brief time.

The intake of carbohydrates depends much on your age, weight, gender and way of life but, in most cases, the keto diet recommends limiting the intake to 20-30 net grams per day. Fats should represent more than 80 percent of your meals, and proteins 15-20 percent.

If you are a beginner, then you can always start with the moderate version of the keto diet, where you are slowly going to cut the carbs from your diet, in case you are afraid that the drastic change of your eating habits can be difficult for you.

What is MEAL PREP?

A SOLUTION IN THE ERA OF A CONSTANT RUSH

Meal Prep or Meal Preparation is about cooking dishes in advance for a few days or a week in order to save time and streamline your healthy eating habits. The idea is to cook a big portion of one type of food and divide it into parts, pack into plastic containers and store in the fridge or freezer.

Meal Prep is very helpful for everyone: busy people find it easier to cook dinner once a week, because they simply have too tight schedule during the week-days; sportsmen cook in advance in order to control intakes of fats, proteins, carbohydrates; dieting individuals monitor their calories intake; people on a low budget prefer Meal Prep, because it is the most economical way of eating. This list can be endless because Meal Prep is a versatile tool to schedule your breakfast, lunches, and dinners, as well as make your nutrition more wholesome.

When you prepare your meals in advance, you will never skip your breakfast just because you overslept and are late for work. You will forget about eating cheap fast food during the day because you will have your homemade healthy lunch box. And finally, Meal Prep will make your evenings better: instead of cooking your dinner after work in more than an hour, you will be able to enjoy the tasty dish as soon as you get home.

WHAT ARE THE BENEFITS FOR YOU?

From planning meals to planning life

A great positive side effect of meal prepping is that you learn how to better organize your life.

The first step is to carefully plan your shopping. If you have never used shopping lists before, it's perhaps time to start. That will help you adjust meals and portions accordingly. You will learn how to prepare and eat just enough without having leftovers or overeating. If you prepare meals for the whole family, you will save yourself the trouble of preparing different food two or even three times a day and then cleaning it all up. The alternative is eating out, but that's expensive and, most of the time, unhealthy.

Planning your meals develops you as a person because once taken care of, that skill may go beyond cooking and will surely help you better organize your life.

The long desired weight loss is finally easy to achieve

Now, when you have the whole-day schedule prepared, you are less likely to snack outside the table. Having a general plan for anything in life actively builds a sense of discipline.

Therefore, if you combine meal prepping with appropriate nutrition, you will create an exceptional lifestyle where weight loss is not a goal in itself, but merely a means to an end. You will not have to obsessively focus on counting, yet you will see results soon enough. No more calories count, weight loss, or how I refer to it as to stay fit, will be easier than ever.

Losing weight happens automatically as an immediate effect of eating proper, schedule-based meals.

Eat Clean! No room for junk food anymore

Through organizing your meals, you decrease the risk of snacking on unhealthy, processed food and fast food tempting you from every corner of the city.

When you have your meals prepared, you quickly notice that even if you fancy some grab-and-go tacos or a burger, you will not go for it. Getting food from vending machines will also become a thing of the past. This is because you are less likely to throw out something you spent time and money on.

You will quickly realize that meal prep helps you be healthier. When you organize your eating habits, you feel better, more energetic, disciplined and not only that you have a sense of control over your life, but this type of food prepping is also the key to long-term happiness. Think of the food as your fuel and of yourself as a top class luxurious car. Would you fuel it with low-quality gas that could damage the engine? Probably not. Meal prepping allows you to skip low-quality fuel and treat your engine better.

Nutritional education

If you want to become an excellent meal planner, basic knowledge about food will come in very handy. Knowing how to compose a balanced meal is not that difficult. A proper content of proteins, fats, and carbohydrates in an adequate ratio will help you remain satiated for a longer period. As a result, hunger pangs will diminish, and you will stop snacking on foods your body doesn't need.

You will not only develop a genuine interest in healthy eating habits, but you will be challenged to learn how to properly pack and store food. Simple as it sounds, a bit of know-how is necessary.

Last but not least, labeling pre-made meals will keep your food organized and make sure you have control over the freshness. Meal prepping does not mean eating stale food.

TIPS FOR A GREAT START

Plan, Pick a day and stick to it

Sunday is considered the best day to prepare food for the whole week.

Draw up a list of meals and days on a piece of paper. That never fails. You can easily print meal planners from the internet, which may be an excellent solution here. Better yet, learn to plan two or even three weeks, and you find the perfect balance and meal prepping days for you.

Go for diversity

That means not repeating the same dish seven times a week. It would be too dull and unhealthy at the same time. Prepare two to three alternatives so you can avoid nutritional burn-out. It may be something as simple as changing the source of proteins (i.e., meat for fish or tofu) or a different type of vegetables.

Make a list before shopping

This will train you to stick to the plan, not toss impulse items into your cart. You will save money and time and keep yourself from buying junk food, however crispy it may be. If something's not in your fridge, you will not eat it.

Keep it simple

Although trying more difficult recipes is most welcome, I recommend that you stick to simple recipes at the beginning. Over time, as you become more adept, you may increase the complexity or try your recipes.

Cook more items at once, whenever possible

An excellent example of that would be roasting a couple of things in the oven or on the stove. It's not only time saving, but your electricity bill will look way better.

Invest in good-quality containers and mason jars

These will help you store things longer without the risk of wasting food, plus they look fancy. Eating from such containers even makes things taste better.

I would also recommend buying larger pots and frying pans.

Buy pre-cut vegetables

Even though they may be a bit more expensive, they make your life easier and will save you additional time and efforts.

Drink lots of water

Very often we confuse hunger pangs with dehydration. Water fills your stomach, and you do not feel hunger, which is why every diet recommends that you drink plenty of water.

WHAT TO AVOID

- Processed and/or packaged foods like pasta, certain types of cheese, pizzas

- Processed and/or packaged meat

- Vegetable oils

- Soft drinks and sugary beverages

- All kinds of crackers, cookies, cakes, and pastries

- Candy bars

- All types of fast foods, including French Fries and Chips

- White bread made of processed white wheat-flour

- Margarine

- Energy drinks

- Ice creams

- MSG and other toxic additives

ALL THINGS ARE DIFFICULT BEFORE THEY BECOME EASY

Going keto while being vegetarian and maintain a healthy lifestyle in a rushing environment, is pretty damn difficult. That's why I created this book, to offer you my wisdom of not taking the easy way out and eating the junk food tempting you everywhere you go. Instead, to learn to take responsibility for what you eat and what you become as a result.

Given all this, the Keto diet offers one of the best possibilities to eat healthy without losing time and energy cooking every day, even twice a day.

These keto vegetarian recipes are meant to help you initiate the changes and go through the tough beginning. But remember, things seem complicated until you make them easy. The results will be well worth the time - no doubt about it.

This book is an investment that pays huge interests quickly without forcing you to spend a lot of money at the beginning. It's effortless to follow, and the results are guaranteed.

Your success is entirely dependent on your determination to stick to the plan and give up on toxic things you considered normal before.

The Keto Recipes in the book are predominantly easy and perfect for beginners. Advanced cooking freaks will find something for themselves as well.

As Buddha said, "to enjoy good health, to bring true happiness to one's family, to bring peace to all, one must first discipline and control one's mind." To take any action, we first need to realize the importance of our diet and how it affects the temples our bodies are. Love the life you have while enjoying the journey to better and healthier nutrition.

WHAT TO EXPECT FROM THIS COOKBOOK

The pages of this cookbook will be guiding you through the whole process of Meal prep, how to follow the Keto Diet and how to get the most out of both using your electric pressure cooker. You will learn how to organize yourself, get everything ready, and what the actual cooking process looks like.

You will learn what meal prep is and how it will transform the way that you eat. Furthermore, I will explain how to get on this journey without feeling overwhelmed or unmotivated. Next, you will learn everything you need to know about the Ketogenic Diet - its' pros and cons. I will also give you reasons why your Instant Pot pressure cooker will take your meal prep to the next level, and how you can use it to create awesome, delicious and easy keto meals.

Finally, I will present you plenty of exciting and inspiring keto diet meal prep recipes that will cover all your daily meals and needs, taking you to the extraordinary lifestyle you always dreamed of.

You will also learn plenty of tips that will help you cook your meal prep meals in the most efficient way, and you will also learn how to use your Instant Pot in the best possible way.

So grab your Instant Pot, this keto diet meal prep cookbook, some groceries and let's start the best culinary journey ever - the meal prepping!

Let's get into it!

Breakfasts

CINNAMON & PUMPKIN WAFFLES

Total Time: 25 minutes | **Serves:** 6

Ingredients

⅓ cup butter, melted
1 ½ cups unsweetened almond milk
4 eggs
¼ tsp liquid stevia
½ tsp baking soda
1 ½ cups almond flour
1 tsp cinnamon powder
½ cup pumpkin puree

Directions

Whisk the almond milk, butter, and eggs in a medium bowl. Add the stevia and baking soda and mix.

Stir in the almond flour and cinnamon powder and combine until no lumps exist. Gently fold in the pumpkin puree until incorporated. Grease waffle iron with cooking spray.

Ladle a ¼ cup of the batter into the waffle iron and close the lid. Cook for 5 minutes until lightly golden. Repeat with the remaining batter. Slice the waffles into quarters.

Storing

Place 2 waffle quarters in different airtight containers for up to 7 days in the fridge.

To freeze, place the waffles in Ziploc bags in the freezer for up to 3 months. Defrost in the microwave for a minute.

Nutritional Fact per Serving:

Calories: 266; Fat: 22.3g; Net Carbs: 7g; Protein: 9.5g

BROCCOLI & RED BELL PEPPER TART

Total Time: 60 minutes | **Serves:** 6

Ingredients

12 eggs
1 ½ cups mozzarella cheese, shredded
1 ½ cups almond milk
½ tsp dried thyme
Salt to taste
1 red bell pepper, sliced
½ cup broccoli, chopped
1 clove garlic, minced

For the Tart

¾ cup almond flour
A pinch of salt
2 oz cold butter
1 tbsp cold water
2 eggs

Directions

Preheat the oven to 400°F. Make breadcrumbs by rubbing the butter into the almond flour and salt in a large bowl. Add the cold water and two eggs and mix everything until dough is formed. Press it into a greased baking dish and refrigerate for 25 minutes.

Meanwhile, beat the 12 eggs with the almond milk, thyme, and salt, then, stir in the bell pepper, broccoli, and garlic. Set aside.

Take out the dough from the fridge and prick it with a fork. Bake in the oven for 20 minutes until pale gold. Spread the mozzarella cheese in the pie crust and top with the egg mixture. Bake in the oven for 30 minutes until the tart is set. Remove and slice into six pieces when cooled.

Storing

Divide between airtight containers and place in the fridge. You can keep them for up to 3 days. To freeze, transfer to Ziploc bags and freeze up to 3 months. Defrost in the microwave for a couple of minutes.

Nutritional Fact per Serving:

Calories: 290; Fat: 18.3g; Net Carbs: 7.3g; Protein: 22.6g

COCONUT BLINI WITH BERRY DRIZZLE

Total Time: 40 minutes | **Serves:** 6

Ingredients

Pancakes

1 cup cream cheese
1 cup coconut flour
1 tsp salt
2 tsp xylitol
1 tsp baking soda

1 tsp baking powder
1½ cups coconut milk
1 tsp vanilla extract
6 large eggs
¼ cup olive oil

Blackberry Sauce

3 cups fresh blackberries
1 lemon, juiced
½ cup xylitol

½ tsp arrowroot starch
A pinch of salt

Directions

Put the coconut flour, salt, xylitol, baking soda, and baking powder in a mixing bowl and whisk to combine. Add in the coconut milk, cream cheese, vanilla, eggs, and olive oil and continue whisking until smooth.

Set a nonstick pan over medium heat and pour a small ladle of batter into the pan; make sure that the batter covers all the surface of the pan. Cook on one side for 2 minutes, flip the blini, and cook the other side for 2 minutes. Transfer to a plate and repeat the cooking process until the batter is exhausted.

Pour the berries and half cup of water into a saucepan, and bring to a boil. Simmer the berries for 12 minutes so that they are soft and exuding juice. Pour in the xylitol at this point, stir, and continue cooking for 5 minutes. Stir in salt and lemon juice.

Mix the arrowroot starch with 1 tablespoon of water; pour the mixture into the berries. Stir and continue cooking the sauce to thicken to your desire. Let it cool.

Storing

Place the blini and berry drizzle in different airtight containers and store for up to 7 days in the fridge.

Nutritional Fact per Serving:

Calories: 433; Fat: 39.7g; Net Carbs: 4.9g; Protein: 8.2g

BUTTERNUT SQUASH & ZUCCHINI LOAF CAKE

Total Time: 70 minutes | **Serves:** 4

Ingredients

5 large eggs
½ cup sour cream
1 cup butternut squash, grated
1 cup zucchini, squeezed and grated
⅓ cup coconut flour
1 tbsp olive oil
¾ tsp baking powder
1 tbsp cinnamon powder
½ tsp salt
1 tsp vinegar
½ tsp nutmeg powder

Directions

Preheat oven to 360°F and grease and line a loaf pan with baking parchment.

In a bowl, put the coconut flour, baking powder, cinnamon powder, salt, and nutmeg. In a separate bowl, whisk together eggs, olive oil, sour cream, and vinegar until combined.

Add the butternut squash and zucchini. Fold the dry mixture into the wet mixture. Pour the batter into the loaf pan and bake for 55 minutes until a skewer comes out clean. Let cool before slicing.

Storing

Place the cake slices in a resealable container and store for up to 5 days at room temperature. To freeze, place in Ziploc bags for up to 3 months. Defrost at room temperature.

Nutritional Fact per Serving:

Calories: 186; Fat: 12.6g; Net Carbs: 7.5g; Protein: 9.5g

SPINACH & CHEESE CUPS

Total Time: 30 minutes | **Serves:** 4

Ingredients

1 cup mascarpone cheese, at room temperature
4 tbsp olive oil
2 cups almond flour
2 tsp baking soda
½ tsp salt
1 egg
1 cup unsweetened almond milk

Directions

Preheat oven to 380°F and spritz a muffin tray with cooking spray. Mix the almond flour, baking soda, and salt in a large bowl. In a separate bowl, beat the mascarpone cheese and olive oil and whisk in the egg and almond milk. Fold in the flour, and spoon 2 tablespoons of the batter into each muffin cup.

Bake for 15-20 minutes until puffy at the top and golden brown, remove to a wire rack to cool slightly for 5 minutes before storing.

Storing

Place the muffins in a resealable container and store for up to 7 days at room temperature.

To freeze, place in Ziploc bags for up to 3 months. Defrost at room temperature.

Nutritional Fact per Serving:

Calories: 299; Fat: 26.8g; Net Carbs: 3.2g; Protein: 11.5g

BRESAOLA & MOZZARELLA SCRAMBLED EGGS

Total Time: 15 minutes | **Serves:** 3

Ingredients

6 eggs
A bunch of fresh chives, chopped
2 ounces mozzarella cheese
1 tbsp butter
1 tbsp water
4 thin slices bresaola
Salt and black pepper, to taste

Directions

Crack the eggs into a large bowl and whisk with the water, salt and pepper. Melt the butter in a skillet and cook the eggs, stirring constantly for 30 seconds. Spread the bresaola slices over and top with mozzarella.

Stir and cook for about 3 minutes until omelet is set. Sprinkle with fresh chives and let cool.

Storing

Divide the scrambled eggs between 4 airtight containers and put in the fridge. Use for up to 3 days.

To freeze, transfer to Ziploc bags and freeze up to 3 months. Defrost in the microwave for a couple of minutes.

Nutritional Fact per Serving:

Calories: 224; Fat: 15g; Net Carbs: 2.2g; Protein: 19g

Poultry Recipes

BROCCOLI & CHEESE CHICKEN CASSEROLE

Total Time: 30 minutes | **Serves:** 4

Ingredients

1 lb chicken breasts, skinless and boneless
Salt and black pepper to season
2 cups broccoli
3 tsp canola oil
4 oz feta cheese, cubed
1 ¼ cups cheddar cheese, shredded
4 tbsp water

Directions

Preheat oven to 370°F and lightly grease a casserole baking dish with cooking spray.

Cut the chicken breasts into bite-sized pieces and sprinkle with salt and black pepper.

Put in the casserole dish and layer broccoli over. Mix the oil with feta cheese and cheddar, and stir in water, 1 tablespoon at a time.

Pour the mixture over the broccoli and cover the pot with aluminium foil.

Bake for 20 minutes, remove foil and continue cooking for 5 minutes until a nice golden brown color is formed on top. Let cool completely before storing.

Storing

Divide between 4 airtight containers or Ziploc bags and refrigerate for up to 3 days.

To freeze, transfer to Ziploc bags and freeze up to 3 months. Defrost in the microwave for a couple of minutes to enjoy.

Nutritional Fact per Serving:

Calories: 452 kcal; Fat: 31.9g; Net Carbs: 2.5g; Protein: 37g

SPANISH PAELLA VALENCIANA "KETO-STYLE"

Total Time: 63 minutes | **Serves:** 4

Ingredients

½ pound chicken drumsticks
½ pound rabbit, cut into pieces
1 white onion, chopped
2 garlic cloves, minced
1 red bell pepper, cut into chunks
2 tbsp olive oil
½ cup thyme, chopped
1 tsp smoked paprika
2 tbsp tomato puree
½ cup white wine
1 cup chicken broth
2 cups cauli rice
1 cup green beans, chopped
A pinch of saffron
Salt and pepper, to taste

Directions

Preheat the oven to 350°F and warm the oil in a pan over medium heat. Season the chicken and rabbit with salt and pepper. Fry in batches on all sides for 8 minutes until lightly brown; remove to a plate.

Add the onion and garlic to the hot oil in the same pan, and sauté for 4 minutes. Include the tomato puree, bell pepper, and paprika, and let simmer for 2 minutes.

Add the broth, and bring the ingredients to a boil for 6 minutes until slightly reduced.

Stir in the cauli rice, white wine, green beans, saffron, and thyme, and lay the meat on top. Transfer the pan to the oven and cook for 20 minutes. Let the paella cool for 10 minutes before storing.

Storing

When cooled, divide between 4 airtight containers and place in the fridge. Consume within 3 days. To freeze, transfer to Ziploc bags and freeze up to 3 months.

Nutritional Fact per Serving:

Calories: 378; Fat: 20.8g; Net Carbs: 7.6g; Protein: 37.2g

EFFORTLESS CHICKEN CHILI

Total Time: 30 minutes | **Serves:** 4

Ingredients

1 tbsp butter
1 tbsp sesame oil
¼ tsp ginger, ground
4 chicken tenders, skinless, boneless, cubed
1 onion, chopped
2 cups chicken broth
8 oz diced tomatoes
2 oz tomato paste
1 tbsp cumin
½ tbsp garlic powder
1 red chili pepper, minced
½ cup shredded cheddar cheese
Salt and black pepper to taste

Directions

Set a large pan over medium heat and add the chicken. Cover with water and bring to a boil. Cook until no longer pink, for 10 minutes. Transfer the chicken to a flat surface to shred with forks.

In a large pot, pour in the butter and sesame oil, and sauté the onion and ginger for 5 minutes. Stir in the chicken, tomatoes, cumin, red chili pepper, garlic powder, tomato paste, and broth.

Adjust the seasoning and bring the mixture to a boil. Reduce heat and simmer for about 10 minutes.

Divide the chicken chili between bowls and top with the cheddar cheese to serve.

Storing

When cooled, divide between 4 airtight jars. Place in the fridge and consume within 3-4 days.

To freeze, divide among 4 freezer-safe containers and place in the freezer. Consume within 3 months. Defrost in the fridge overnight and heat for a few minutes.

Nutritional Fact per Serving:

Calories: 396; Fat: 22.9g; Net Carbs: 5.7g; Protein: 38.7g

BRAISED CHICKEN THIGHS WITH TOMATOES & EGGPLANT

Total Time: 45 minutes | **Serves:** 4

Ingredients

2 green onions, chopped
2 cloves garlic, minced
2 tbsp butter
1 lb chicken thighs
Kosher salt and black pepper to taste
2 cups canned tomatoes, chopped
1 eggplant, cubed
2 tbsp fresh basil, chopped

Directions

Season the chicken with salt and black pepper. Melt butter in a saucepan over medium heat, and fry the chicken, skin side down, for 4 minutes until golden. Flip and cook for another 2 minutes; remove to a plate.

In the same saucepan, sauté the garlic and onions for 3 minutes, add in the eggplant and cook for 5 minutes until brown and soft. Stir in tomatoes and cook for 10 minutes.

Season the sauce with salt and black pepper, stir and add the chicken. Coat with sauce and simmer for 10-15 minutes. Garnish with basil and let sit until completely cooled.

Storing

When cooled, divide between 4 airtight containers. Place in the fridge. You can use them for up to 3 days.

To freeze, transfer to Ziploc bags and freeze up to 3 months. Defrost in the microwave for a few minutes.

Nutritional Fact per Serving:

Calories: 366; Fat: 25.2g; Net Carbs: 6.9g; Protein: 21.5g

CHICKEN THIGHS WITH GREENS

Total Time: 20 minutes | **Serves:** 4

Ingredients

4 chicken thighs
1 cup spinach, chopped
½ cup celery leaves, chopped
½ cup Swiss chard, chopped
1 tsp parsley
1 cup half-and-half
1 cup vegetable broth
4 tbsp butter

Directions

Melt half of the butter in a skillet and brown the chicken on all sides, about 8 minutes. Set aside.

Add the remaining butter. Whisk in half-and-half, bring to a boil, and stir in the parsley.

Add the spinach, Swiss chard, and celery to the skillet and cook until wilted. Add the thighs in the skillet and cook for another 6 minutes.

Storing

When cooled, divide between 4 airtight containers or Ziploc bags and place in the fridge. You can use them for up to 3 days.

To freeze, transfer to Ziploc bags and freeze up to 3 months.

Nutritional Fact per Serving:

Calories: 558; Fat: 43.7g; Net Carbs: 5.7g; Protein: 35g

CHEESE-CRUSTED CHICKEN BREASTS

Total Time: 40 minutes | **Serves:** 4

Ingredients

3 tbsp olive oil
3 cups Monterey Jack cheese, shredded
2 eggs
½ cup pork rinds, crushed
1 lb chicken breasts, boneless
Salt to taste

Directions

Line a baking sheet with parchment paper.

Whisk the eggs with the olive oil in one bowl, and mix the cheese and pork rinds in another bowl. Season the chicken with salt, dip in egg mixture, and coat generously in the cheese mixture.

Place on a baking sheet, cover with aluminium foil and bake in the oven for 25 minutes at 350°F.

Remove foil and bake further for 12 minutes until golden brown.

Storing

When cooled, divide between 4 airtight containers or Ziploc bags and place in the fridge for up to 3 days.

To freeze, transfer to Ziploc bags and freeze up to 3 months. Defrost in the microwave and for a few minutes.

Nutritional Fact per Serving:

Calories: 722; Fat: 53.8; Net Carbs: 1.2g; Protein: 45.1g

SHIITAKE CHICKEN IN A SKILLET

Total Time: 35 minutes | **Serves:** 4

Ingredients

1 cup shiitake mushrooms, sliced
4 green onions, sliced
2 garlic cloves, minced
4 tbsp coconut oil
1 tsp Dijon mustard
1 tbsp cilantro, chopped
1 pound chicken thighs
Salt and black pepper, to taste

Directions

Season the thighs with salt and black pepper. Melt the coconut oil in a pan, and cook the chicken until browned, for about 3-4 minutes per side; and set aside.

Add mushrooms, garlic, and green onions to the same oil, and cook for about 5 minutes.

Stir in Dijon mustard and a ½ cup of water.

Return the chicken to the pan, reduce the heat, cover and simmer for 15 minutes. Sprinkle with fresh cilantro and let cool before storing.

Storing

Divide between 4 airtight containers. Place in the fridge and consume within 3 days.

To freeze, transfer to Ziploc bags and freeze up to 3 months. Defrost in the microwave for a couple of minutes to enjoy.

Nutritional Fact per Serving:

Calories: 383; Fat: 32.6g; Net Carbs: 2.9g; Protein: 19.4g

HOT CHICKEN MEATBALL TRAY

Total Time: 25 minutes | **Serves:** 4

Ingredients

1 egg
1 pound ground chicken
Salt and black pepper, to taste
1 red pepper, chopped
2 spring onions, chopped
¼ cup pecorino cheese, grated
1 tbsp dry Italian seasoning
2 tbsp olive oil
¼ cup hot sauce
2 tbsp parsley, chopped

Directions

Preheat oven to 480°F.

In a bowl, combine chicken meat, red pepper, onions, Italian seasoning, pecorino cheese, salt, black pepper, parsley, and egg, and mix with your hands well.

Form into meatballs, arrange them on a greased with olive oil baking tray, and bake in the oven for 16 minutes.

Remove from the oven, into a bowl and cover with hot sauce. Let sit until completely cooled.

Storing

When cooled, divide between 4 airtight containers. Refrigerate and consume within 3 days.

Nutritional Fact per Serving:

Calories: 383; Fat: 28.1g; Net Carbs: 4.4g; Protein: 25.8g

CHICKEN & VEGETABLE BAKE

Total Time: 45 minutes | **Serves:** 4

Ingredients

1 lb chicken breasts, sliced
1 tbsp butter
2 green bell peppers, sliced
1 turnip, chopped
1 onion, chopped
1 zucchini, sliced
2 garlic cloves, minced
2 tsp Italian seasoning
Salt and black pepper to taste
8 oz mozzarella cheese, sliced

Directions

Grease a baking dish with cooking spray and place in the chicken slices.

Melt the butter in a pan over medium heat and sauté the onion, zucchini, garlic, bell peppers, turnip, salt, black pepper, and 1 tsp of Italian seasonings.

Cook until tender, about 8 minutes.

Spread the vegetables over the chicken and cover with cheese slices. Set into the oven and cook until browned for 30 minutes at 370°F.

Storing

When cooled, divide between 4 airtight containers or Ziploc bags and place in the fridge. You can use them for up to 3 days.

To freeze, transfer to Ziploc bags and freeze up to 3 months.

Nutritional Fact per Serving:

Calories: 341; Fat: 13.5g; Net Carbs: 8.3g; Protein: 43g

CHICKEN AND BACON PIE

Total Time: 55 minutes | **Serves:** 4

Ingredients

¾ cup Greek yogurt
1 sweet onion, chopped
3 oz bacon, chopped
3 tbsp butter
1 carrot, chopped

3 garlic cloves, minced
Salt and black pepper, to taste
½ cup chicken stock
½ pound chicken breasts, cubed
¾ cup mozzarella cheese, shredded

For the dough

¾ cup almond flour
3 tbsp cottage cheese
1 ½ cups mozzarella cheese, shredded
1 egg

1 tsp onion powder
1 tsp garlic powder
Salt and black pepper, to taste

Directions

Preheat oven to 370°F. Sauté the onion, garlic, black pepper, bacon, salt, and carrot, for 5 minutes in warm butter over medium heat. Add in the chicken, and cook for 3 minutes.

Stir in the Greek yogurt, and stock, and cook for 7 minutes. Add in the mozzarella cheese and set aside.

Using a bowl, combine the mozzarella cheese with the cottage cheese, and heat in a microwave for 1 minute. Stir in the garlic powder, salt, almond flour, black pepper, onion powder, and egg.

Knead the dough well, split into 4 pieces, and flatten each into a circle. Set the chicken mixture into 4 ramekins, top each with a dough circle, and bake in the oven for 25 minutes.

Storing

Cover with plastic wrap and place in the fridge. You can use them for up to 3 days.

To freeze, cover with aluminium foil and freeze for up to 3 months. Defrost in the microwave for a couple of minutes to enjoy.

Nutritional Fact per Serving:

Calories: 503; Fat: 30.5g; Net Carbs: 5.6g; Protein: 40.9g

SWEET ONION CHICKEN WITH COCONUT SAUCE

Total Time: 35 minutes | **Serves:** 6

Ingredients

1 tbsp coconut oil
3 chicken breasts, halved
1 cup vegetable stock
2 sweet onions, very thinly sliced
1 lime, juiced
2 oz coconut cream
1 tsp red pepper flakes
1 tbsp fresh cilantro, chopped
Salt and ground black pepper, to taste

Directions

Cook the chicken in hot coconut oil, in a pan over medium heat, for about 4-5 minutes; set aside.

Place the sweet onions in the pan and cook for 4 minutes. Stir in black pepper, stock, pepper flakes, salt, coconut cream, and lime juice.

Return the chicken to the pan, and cook covered for 15 minutes.

Sprinkle with fresh cilantro and let cool.

Storing

When cooled, divide between 6 airtight containers and refrigerate for up to 3 days.

To freeze, transfer to Ziploc bags and freeze up to 3 months. Defrost in the microwave for a couple of minutes to enjoy.

Nutritional Fact per Serving:

Calories: 481; Fat: 27.5g; Net Carbs: 5.2g; Protein: 39g

CHARGRILLED CHILI CHICKEN

Total Time: 17 minutes | **Serves:** 6

Ingredients

3 tbsp chili powder
Salt and black pepper to taste
2 tsp garlic powder
2 tbsp olive oil
1 ½ pounds chicken breasts

Directions

Grease grill grate with cooking spray and preheat to 400°F.

Combine chili powder, salt, black pepper, and garlic powder in a bowl.

Brush chicken with olive oil, sprinkle with spice mixture and massage with hands.

Grill for 7 minutes per side until well-cooked; then let cool.

Storing

Divide the eggs between 6 airtight containers. Place in the fridge for 3 days.

To freeze, transfer to Ziploc bags and freeze up to 3 months. Serve with steamed broccoli or asparagus.

Nutritional Fact per Serving:

Calories: 253; Fat: 15.6g; Net Carbs: 1.8g. Protein: 24.5g

MUSTARD CHICKEN CASSEROLE WITH PANCETTA

Total Time: 40 minutes | **Serves:** 4

Ingredients

3 oz smoked pancetta, chopped
5 tbsp Dijon mustard
1 fennel bulb, trimmed and sliced
Salt and black pepper, to taste
1 onion, chopped
2 tbsp olive oil
1 cup chicken stock
1 pound chicken breasts, skinless and boneless
¼ tsp sweet paprika
1 tbsp tarragon, chopped

Directions

Put the mustard in a bowl and add in the sweet paprika, salt, and black pepper; stir to combine. Rub the mixture onto all chicken sides and massage.

Warm half of the olive oil in a casserole over medium heat and cook the chicken for 2-3 minutes per side until golden. Set aside.

To the same casserole, add the remaining olive oil and cook the pancetta, onion, and fennel for 5 minutes.

Return the chicken, pour over the stock, and bring to a simmer for 20 minutes, turning the meat halfway through.

Taste and adjust the seasoning, sprinkle with tarragon and let cool at room temperature.

Storing

Divide between 4 airtight containers and put in the fridge. You can use them for up to 3 days.

To freeze, transfer to Ziploc bags and freeze up to 3 months. Defrost in the microwave for a few minutes to enjoy.

Nutritional Fact per Serving:

Calories: 368; Fat: 24.2g; Net Carbs: 2.5g; Protein: 28.4g

CREAMY CHICKEN WITH MUSHROOMS

Total Time: 40 minutes | **Serves:** 4

Ingredients

2 tbsp olive oil
2 garlic cloves, minced
1 onion, sliced into half-moons
1 cup mushrooms, chopped
1 tbsp sweet paprika
1 cup chicken stock
¼ cup dry white wine
1 cup heavy cream
4 chicken breasts, sliced
2 tbsp fresh parsley, chopped
Salt and black pepper, to taste

Directions

Heat the olive oil in a saucepan over medium heat and sauté the onion and garlic for 3 minutes until soft. Remove to a plate. Add in the chicken and fry until lightly browned, for about 5 minutes.

Pour in the white wine, mushrooms and paprika, salt, and black pepper, and cook for 3-4 minutes until the liquid is reduced by half.

Return the sautéed onion and garlic, and add in the stock. Cook for 20 minutes, then stir in the heavy cream and cook for 2 more minutes. Scatter the fresh parsley and let cool before storing.

Storing

Divide between 4 airtight containers. Place in the fridge and consume within 3-4 days.

To freeze, transfer to Ziploc bags and freeze up to 3 months. Defrost in the microwave for a couple of minutes to enjoy.

Nutritional Fact per Serving:

Calories: 485; Fat: 25.8g; Net Carbs: 3.4g; Protein: 56.7g

ROSEMARY CHICKEN AND PUMPKIN BAKE

Total Time: 60 minutes | **Serves:** 4

Ingredients

1 pound chicken thighs
1 pound pumpkin, cubed
½ cup black olives, pitted
A bunch of spring onions, sliced
½ tsp ground cinnamon
¼ tsp ground nutmeg
4 tbsp olive oil
5 garlic cloves, sliced
1 tbsp dried rosemary
Salt and black pepper, to taste

Directions

Set oven to 400°F and grease a baking dish with cooking spray.

Place in the chicken with the skin down. Set the garlic, olives, spring onions, and pumpkin around the chicken, then drizzle with olive oil.

Season with black pepper, salt, cinnamon, nutmeg and rosemary over the mixture, and insert in the oven. Cook for 45 minutes.

Storing

Divide the kale between 4 airtight containers. Place in the fridge and consume within 3-4 days.

To freeze, transfer to Ziploc bags and freeze up to 3 months. Defrost in the microwave for a few minutes to enjoy.

Nutritional Fact per Serving:

Calories: 431; Fat: 34.2g; Net Carbs: 6.1g; Protein: 20.5g

BELL PEPPER TURKEY KETO CARNITAS

Total Time: 25 minutes | **Serves:** 4

Ingredients

1 lb turkey breasts, skinless, boneless, sliced
1 garlic clove, minced
1 red onion, sliced
1 green chili, minced
2 tsp ground cumin
2 tbsp lime juice
Salt and black pepper, to taste
1 tsp sweet paprika
2 tbsp olive oil
1 tsp ground coriander
1 green bell pepper, seeded, sliced
1 red bell pepper, seeded, sliced
1 tbsp fresh cilantro, chopped

Directions

Using a bowl, combine lime juice, cumin, garlic, coriander, sweet paprika, salt, green chili, and black pepper. Toss in the turkey pieces to coat well.

Set a pan over medium heat and warm oil. Place in the turkey and cook each side for 3 minutes; set aside in a plate.

In the same pan, sauté the bell peppers, cilantro, and onion for 6 minutes, until soft. Transfer over the turkey and let cool completely. Serve in lettuce leaves

Storing

Divide between 6 airtight containers. Place in the fridge and consume within 3 days.

To freeze, transfer to Ziploc bags and freeze up to 3 months. Defrost in the microwave for a couple of minutes to enjoy.

Nutritional Fact per Serving:

Calories: 262; Fat: 15.2g; Net Carbs: 4.2g; Protein: 25.8g

CREAMY TURKEY & BROCCOLI BAKE

Total Time: 30 minutes | **Serves:** 4

Ingredients

1 lb turkey breasts, cooked
2 tbsp butter, melted
1 head broccoli, cut into florets
½ cup buttermilk
1 carrot, sliced
½ cup heavy cream
1 cup cheddar cheese, grated
4 tbsp pork rinds, crushed
Salt and black pepper, to taste
1 tsp oregano

Directions

Grease and line a baking pan. Boil water in a pot. Add in broccoli and cook for 3-4 minutes until tender.

Shred the turkey and place into a large bowl together with buttermilk, butter, oregano, carrot, and broccoli; mix to combine. Season with salt and black pepper, and transfer the mixture to the baking pan.

Sprinkle with heavy cream over the dish and top with grated cheese. Cover with the pork rinds. Place in the oven and cook until bubbling for 20-25 minutes at 450°F. When ready, let cool completely.

Storing

When cooled, divide between 4 airtight containers. Place in the fridge and consume within 4 days.

To freeze, divide among 4 Ziploc bags and place in the freezer. Consume within 3 months. Defrost in the fridge overnight and heat for a few minutes.

Nutritional Fact per Serving:

Calories: 469; Fat: 31.5g; Net Carbs: 6.2g; Protein: 38.4g

ROSEMARY TURKEY CAKES & BALSAMIC BRUSSELS SPROUTS

Total Time: 35 minutes | **Serves:** 4

Ingredients

For the burgers

1 pound ground turkey
1 egg
1 onion, chopped
1 garlic clove, minced
Salt and black pepper to taste
1 tsp fresh rosemary, chopped
4 tbsp olive oil

For the fried Brussels sprouts

1 ½ lb Brussels sprouts
4 tbsp olive oil
2 tbsp balsamic vinegar
Salt to taste

Directions

Preheat oven to 320°F and arrange the Brussels sprouts in a baking dish. Toss to coat with the olive oil, and season with salt. Bake in the oven for about 20 minutes, stirring once.

Then, pour the vinegar over and cook for 5 more minutes. Combine the burger ingredients in a mixing bowl. Form patties out of the mixture. Set a large pan over medium heat, warm the olive oil, and fry the patties until cooked through.

Storing

When cooled, divide between 4 airtight containers. Place in the fridge and consume within 3 days.

Nutritional Fact per Serving:

Calories: 535; Fat: 38.7g; Net Carbs: 5.7g; Protein: 31g

COCONUT TURKEY CHILI

Total Time: 30 minutes | **Serves:** 4

Ingredients

1 pound turkey breasts, cubed
1 cup broccoli, chopped
2 shallots, sliced
1 (14-ounce) can tomatoes, diced
2 tbsp coconut oil
2 tbsp coconut cream
2 garlic cloves, minced
1 tbsp ground coriander
2 tbsp fresh ginger, grated
1 tbsp turmeric
1 tbsp cumin
Salt and black pepper, to taste
2 tbsp chili powder

Directions

Melt coconut oil in a pan over medium heat and stir-fry the turkey and shallots for 5 minutes. Place in garlic and ginger, and cook for another minute.

Stir in tomatoes, broccoli, black pepper, turmeric, coriander, salt, cumin, and chili powder. Pour in the coconut cream, and cook for 10 minutes.

Transfer to a food processor to blend well. Simmer for 15 minutes, then let to cool at room temperature.

Storing

When cooled, divide between 4 rigid containers, leaving a little space for expansion. Place in the fridge and consume within 3 days.

To freeze, transfer to Ziploc bags and freeze up to 3 months. Defrost in the microwave and microwave for a couple of minutes to enjoy.

Nutritional Fact per Serving:

Calories: 318; Fat: 18.7g; Net Carbs: 6.6g; Protein: 27.7g

LEFTOVER TURKEY STEW

Total Time: 20 minutes | **Serves:** 4

Ingredients

4 cups leftover from roasted turkey, chopped
2 cups green bell peppers, sliced
1 red onion sliced
2 garlic cloves, minced
1 tbsp olive oil
24 oz chicken stock
Salt and black pepper, to taste
1 tbsp chipotle chilli paste
½ cup spinach, chopped
1 tsp ground coriander
2 tsp cumin
¼ cup sour cream
1 tbsp fresh cilantro, chopped

Directions

Warm olive oil in a saucepan over medium heat. Cook in the onion and garlic for 3 minutes until fragrant.

Stir in the chicken stock, bell peppers, and bring to a boil, then simmer for 10 minutes covered.

Place in the leftover turkey, spinach, ground coriander, chipotle chilli paste, cumin, and black pepper; simmer for 5 minutes. Stir in the sour cream, and top with cilantro.

Storing

When cooled, divide between 4 airtight containers. Place in the fridge and consume within 3 days.

To freeze, transfer to Ziploc bags and freeze up to 3 months. Defrost in the microwave for a few minutes.

Nutritional Fact per Serving:

Calories: 473; Fat: 21.5g; Net Carbs: 1.7g; Protein: 63g

Red Meat Recipes

SWEET PORK CHOPS WITH BBQ SAUCE

Total Time: 2 hours 20 minutes | **Serves:** 4

Ingredients

4 oz BBQ sauce, sugar-free
1 ¼ pounds pork chops
Salt and black pepper to taste
1 tbsp xylitol
½ tsp ginger powder
2 tsp smoked paprika

Directions

Preheat the grill to 450°F.

In a bowl, mix the black pepper, xylitol, ginger powder, and smoked paprika, and rub the pork chops on all sides with the mixture. Then, cover the pork chops with plastic wraps and place them in the refrigerator to marinate for 2 hours.

Unwrap the meat, place on the grill grate, and cook for 2 minutes per side. Reduce the heat and brush the BBQ sauce on the meat, cover and grill for 5 minutes.

Open the lid, turn the meat and brush again with BBQ sauce. Continue cooking covered for 5 minutes. Remove the meat to a serving platter and let cool.

Storing

When cooled, divide between 4 airtight containers and place in the fridge Best if consumed within 3 days.

To freeze, transfer to Ziploc bags and freeze up to 3 months. Defrost in the microwave for a few minutes.

Nutritional Fact per Serving:

Calories: 352; Fat: 22.9g; Net Carbs: 2.5g; Protein: 37g

BASIL PORK MEATBALLS IN TOMATO SAUCE

Total Time: 45 minutes | **Serves:** 6

Ingredients

1 pound ground pork
2 green onions, chopped
1 tbsp olive oil
1 cup pork rinds, crushed
3 cloves garlic, minced
½ cup buttermilk
2 eggs, beaten
1 cup asiago cheese, shredded
Salt and black pepper to taste
1 can (29-ounce) tomato sauce, sugar-free
1 cup pecorino cheese, grated
Chopped basil to garnish

Directions

Preheat the oven to 370°F.

Mix together the buttermilk, ground pork, garlic, asiago cheese, eggs, salt, black pepper, and pork rinds in a bowl, until combined. Shape the pork mixture into balls and place them into an oiled baking pan. Cook in the oven for 20 minutes.

Remove from the oven. Pour the tomato sauce all over and sprinkle with the pecorino cheese.

Cover the pan with foil and put it back in the oven to cook for 10 minutes. Remove the foil, and continue cooking for 5 minutes. Once ready, take out the pan and garnish with basil.

Storing

Divide between 4 airtight containers. Place in the fridge and consume within 3 days.

To freeze, transfer to Ziploc bags and freeze up to 3 months. Defrost in the microwave for a couple of minutes to enjoy.

Nutritional Fact per Serving:

Calories: 623; Fat: 51.8g; Net Carbs: 4.6g; Protein: 53g

MUSHROOM & PORK CASSEROLE

Total Time: 38 minutes | **Serves:** 4

Ingredients

1 cup ricotta cheese, crumbled
1 cup Italian cheese blend
4 carrots, thinly sliced
Salt and black pepper to taste
1 clove garlic, minced
1 ¼ pounds ground pork
4 green onions, chopped

1 cup portobello mushrooms, chopped
15 oz canned tomatoes
4 tbsp pork rinds, crushed
¼ cup chopped parsley
3 tbsp olive oil
⅓ cup water

Directions

Mix half of the parsley, ricotta cheese, and Italian cheese blend in a bowl. Set aside.

Heat the olive oil in a skillet over medium heat and cook the pork for 3 minutes or until no longer pink. Stir occasionally while breaking any lumps apart.

Add garlic, half of the green onions, mushrooms, and 2 tbsp of pork rinds. Continue cooking for 3 minutes. Stir in the tomatoes, remaining parsley, and water. Cook further for 3 minutes, and then turn the heat off.

Sprinkle the bottom of a baking dish with 2 tbsp of pork rinds; top with half of the carrots and a season of salt, 2/3 of the pork mixture, and the cheese mixture.

Repeat the layering process a second time to exhaust the ingredients. Cover the baking dish with foil and bake for 20 minutes at 370°F.

Remove the foil and brown the top of the casserole with the broiler side of the oven for 2 minutes.

Storing

Divide between 4 airtight containers and put in the fridge. You can use them for up to 3 days.

To freeze, transfer to Ziploc bags and freeze up to 3 months. Defrost in the microwave for a few minutes to enjoy.

Nutritional Fact per Serving:

Calories: 672; Fat: 56.8g; Net Carbs: 7.9g; Protein: 34.8g

TURNIP PORK PIE

Total Time: 50 minutes | **Serves:** 8

Ingredients

1 cup turnip mash
2 pounds ground pork
½ cup water
1 onion, chopped
1 tbsp sage
2 tbsp butter

Crust:

2 oz butter
1 egg
2 oz cheddar, shredded
2 cups almond flour
¼ tsp xanthan gum
A pinch of salt

Directions

Stir together all crust ingredients in a bowl. Make two balls out of the mixture and refrigerate for 10 minutes.

In a pan over medium heat, warm 2 tbsp of butter and sauté the onion and ground pork for 6-8 minutes. Remove to a bowl, let cool for a few minutes and add in the turnip mash and sage. Mix with hands.

Roll out the pie crusts and place one at the bottom of a greased pie pan. Spread the filling over the crust and top with the other coat. Bake in the oven for 30 minutes at 350°F. When ready, let cool to slice.

Storing

Divide between 8 airtight containers and place in the fridge. Best if consumed within 3 days.

To freeze, transfer to Ziploc bags and freeze up to 3 months.

Nutritional Fact per Serving:

Calories: 477; Fat: 36.1g; Net Carbs: 1.7g; Protein: 33g

PORK & BACON PARCELS

Total Time: 40 minutes | **Serves:** 4

Ingredients

4 bacon strips
2 tbsp fresh parsley, chopped
4 pork loin chops, boneless
⅓ cup cottage cheese
1 tbsp olive oil
1 onion, chopped
1 tbsp garlic powder
2 tomatoes, chopped
⅓ cup chicken stock
Salt and black pepper, to taste

Directions

Lay a bacon strip on top of each pork chop, then divide the parsley and cottage cheese on top. Roll each pork piece and secure with toothpicks.

Set a pan over medium heat and warm oil, cook the pork parcels until browned, and remove to a plate. Add in the onion, and cook for 5 minutes. Pour in the chicken stock and garlic powder, and cook for 3 minutes.

Get rid of the toothpicks from the rolls and return them to the pan. Stir in black pepper, salt, parsley, and tomatoes, bring to a boil, set heat to medium-low, and cook for 25 minutes while covered.

Storing

When cooled, divide between 4 airtight containers (or one large if you are planning on serving it all at once). Place in the fridge and consume within 3 days.

To freeze, transfer to Ziploc bags and freeze up to 3 months. Defrost in the microwave and microwave for a couple of minutes to enjoy.

Nutritional Fact per Serving:

Calories: 433; Fat: 23.4g; Net Carbs: 6.8g; Protein: 44.6g

CAULIFLOWER PORK GOULASH

Total Time: 30 minutes | **Serves**: 4

Ingredients

2 tbsp butter
1 cup mushrooms, sliced
1 ½ pounds ground pork
Salt and black pepper, to taste
2 cups cauliflower florets
1 onion, chopped
14 ounces canned diced tomatoes
1 garlic clove, minced
1 tbsp smoked paprika
2 tbsp parsley, chopped
1 tbsp tomato puree
1 ½ cups water

Directions

Melt the butter in a pan over medium heat, stir in the pork, and brown for 5 minutes.

Place in the mushrooms, garlic, and onion, and cook for 4 minutes.

Stir in smoked paprika, water, tomatoes, tomato paste, and cauliflower, bring to a simmer and cook for 20 minutes. Add in black pepper, salt and parsley.

Storing

When cooled, divide between 4 airtight containers. Place in the fridge and consume within 3 days.

Nutritional Fact per Serving:

Calories: 533; Fat: 41.8g; Net Carbs: 7g; Protein: 35.5g

CARIBBEAN JERK PORK

Total Time: 4 hours 20 minutes | **Serves:** 4

Ingredients

1 ½ pounds pork roast
1 tbsp olive oil
¼ cup jerk seasoning
2 tbsp soy sauce, sugar-free
½ cup vegetable stock

Directions

Preheat oven to 350°F and rub the pork with olive oil and jerk seasoning.

Heat olive oil in a pan over medium heat and sear the meat well on all sides, about 4-5 minutes.

Put the pork in a baking dish, add in the vegetable stock and soy sauce, cover with aluminium foil and bake for 45 minutes, turning once halfway.

Then, remove the foil and continue cooking until completely cooked through. Slice when cooled.

Storing

Divide between 4 airtight containers. Place in the fridge and consume within 3 days.

To freeze, transfer to Ziploc bags and freeze up to 3 months. Defrost in the microwave for a couple of minutes to enjoy.

Nutritional Fact per Serving:

Calories: 407; Fat: 20g; Net Carbs: 5.6g; Protein: 45.9g

SAVORY JALAPEÑO PORK MEATBALLS

Total Time: 45 minutes | **Serves:** 4

Ingredients

3 green onions, chopped
1 tbsp garlic powder
1 pound ground pork
1 jalapeño pepper, chopped
1 tsp dried oregano
2 tsp parsley
½ tsp Italian Seasoning
2 tsp cumin

Salt and black pepper, to taste
3 tbsp butter melted + 2 tbsp
4 ounces cream cheese
1 tsp turmeric
¼ tsp xylitol
½ tsp baking powder
1 ½ cups flax meal
½ cup almond flour

Directions

Preheat oven to 350°F. In a food processor, add green onions, garlic powder, jalapeño pepper, and ½ cup water.; blend well.

Set a pan over medium heat, warm in 2 tbsp of butter and cook the ground pork for 3 minutes. Stir in the onion mixture, and cook for 2 minutes.

Stir in parsley, cloves, salt, cumin, ½ teaspoon turmeric, oregano, Italian Seasoning , and black pepper, and cook for 3 minutes.

In a bowl, combine the remaining turmeric, with almond flour, xylitol, flax meal, and baking powder. In a separate bowl, combine the 3 tbsp melted butter with cream cheese.

Combine the 2 mixtures to obtain a dough. Form balls from this mixture, set them on a parchment paper, and roll each into a circle.

Split the pork mixture on one-half of the dough circles, cover with the other half, seal edges, and lay on a lined sheet. Bake for 25 minutes in the oven.

Storing

When cooled, divide between 4 airtight containers. Place in the fridge and consume within 3 days.

Nutritional Fact per Serving:

Calories: 598; Fat: 45.8g; Net Carbs: 5.3g; Protein: 35g

SCOTTISH BEEF STEW

Total Time: 60 minutes | **Serves:** 4

Ingredients

2 tbsp lard
1 ¼ pounds beef chuck roast, cubed
1 parsnip, chopped
1 onion, chopped
12 oz sweet potatoes, cut into quarters
1 clove garlic, minced
Salt and black pepper to taste
1 ½ cups beef stock
2 tsp rosemary, chopped

Directions

Melt the lard in a skillet over medium heat and cook the onion and garlic for 4 minutes. Add in the beef, season with salt and pepper, and brown on all sides, for about 7-8 minutes.

Add sweet potatoes, parsnip, rosemary, and beef stock. Stir and cook on low heat for 35-40 minutes, covered. Let cool completely.

Storing

Divide between 4 airtight containers. Place in the fridge for up to 3 days.

To freeze, transfer to Ziploc bags and freeze up to 3 months. Defrost in the microwave and microwave for a couple of minutes to enjoy.

Nutritional Fact per Serving:

Calories: 445; Fat: 18.6g; Net Carbs: 12.3g; Protein: 41.8g

ASSORTED GRILLED VEGGIES AND BEEF STEAKS

Total Time: 30 minutes | **Serves:** 4

Ingredients

4 tbsp olive oil
1 ¼ pounds sirloin steaks
Salt and black pepper to taste
3 tbsp balsamic vinegar
½ lb asparagus, trimmed
1 eggplant, sliced
2 zucchinis, sliced
1 red bell pepper, cut into strips
1 green bell pepper, cut into strips
1 red onion, sliced

Directions

Divide the meat and vegetables between two bowls. Mix salt, pepper, olive oil, and balsamic vinegar in a small bowl. Rub the beef all over with half of this mixture. Pour the remaining mixture over the vegetables.

Preheat a grill pan over medium heat. Drain the steaks and reserve the marinade. Sear the steaks on the grill on both sides for 8-10 minutes, flipping once halfway through; and set aside.

Pour the vegetables and marinade in the pan; and cook for 5 minutes, turning once. After, let cool completely.

Storing

Divide the cooled steaks between 4 airtight containers and top each with ¼ of the grilled vegetables. Place in the fridge and consume within 3-4 days.

To freeze, transfer to Ziploc bags and freeze up to 1-2 months. Defrost in the microwave and microwave for a couple of minutes to enjoy.

Nutritional Fact per Serving:

Calories: 459; Fat: 30.7g; Net Carbs: 4.5g; Protein: 32.8g

EASY RUMP STEAK SALAD

Total Time: 40 minutes | **Serves:** 4

Ingredients

1 pound flank steak
½ pound Brussels sprouts
3 green onions, sliced
1 cucumber, sliced
1 cup green beans, steamed and sliced
9 oz mixed salad greens
Salt and black pepper to season

Salad Dressing

2 tsp Dijon mustard
1 tsp xylitol
Salt and black pepper to taste
3 tbsp extra virgin olive oil
1 tbsp red wine vinegar

Directions

Preheat a grill pan over high heat. Meanwhile, season the meat with salt and pepper. Brown the steak in the pan for 5 minutes per side. Remove to rest on a chopping board for 5 minutes before slicing thinly.

Put the Brussels sprouts on a baking sheet, drizzle with olive oil and bake in the oven for 25 minutes at 400°F. After cooking, remove, and set aside to cool.

In a bowl, mix the Dijon mustard, xylitol, salt, pepper, vinegar, and olive oil. Set aside.

In a shallow salad bowl, add the green onions, cucumber, green beans, cooled Brussels sprouts, salad greens, and steak slices.

Storing

Divide the undressed salad between 4 airtight containers and put in the fridge. You can use them for up to 5 days. Put the dressing in glass jar fur up to 14 days. Shake the dressing before serving to coat the salad.

Nutritional Fact per Serving:

Calories: 244; Fat: 10.7g; Net Carbs: 3.3g; Protein: 27.4g

GARLICKY ROAST RIB OF BEEF

Total Time: 55 minutes | **Serves:** 6

Ingredients

4 tbsp olive oil
3 pounds beef ribs
3 heads garlic, cut in half
3 onions, halved
2 lemons, zested
A pinch of mustard powder
3 tbsp xylitol
Salt and black pepper to taste
3 tbsp fresh sage leaves
¼ cup water
¼ cup red wine

Directions

Score shallow crisscrosses patterns on the meat.

Mix the xylitol, mustard powder, sage, salt, black pepper, and lemon zest to make a rub; and apply it all over the beef with your hands, particularly into the cuts.

Now, place the garlic heads and onion halves in a baking dish, toss them with olive oil, and cook in the oven for 15 minutes at 410°F.

Place the beef on top of the onion and garlic. Pour in the water and red wine, cover the dish with foil and cook in the oven for 15 minutes.

Remove the foil and continue cooking for 10 minutes. Let cool completely and slice the meat.

Storing

Divide between airtight containers. Place in the fridge for up to 3 days.

To freeze, transfer to Ziploc bags and freeze up to 3 months. Defrost in the microwave and microwave for a couple of minutes to enjoy.

Nutritional Fact per Serving:

Calories: 749 Fat: 65.6g; Net Carbs: 5.5g; Protein: 53g

SPICY CHEESE & KALE PINWHEEL

Total Time: 42 minutes | **Serves:** 4

Ingredients

2 tbsp olive oil
1 pound flank steak
Salt and black pepper to season
1 cup cotija cheese, crumbled
1 cup kale
1 habanero pepper, chopped
2 tbsp cilantro, chopped

Directions

Grease a baking sheet with olive oil. Cover the meat with plastic wrap on a flat surface and flatten it with a mallet. Take off the wraps.

Sprinkle with half of the cheese, top with kale, habanero pepper, cilantro, and the remaining cheese. Roll the steak over on the stuffing and secure with toothpicks.

Place in the baking sheet and cook for 30 minutes at 400°F, flipping once until nicely browned on the outside and the cheese melted within.

Cool for 3 minutes and slice into pinwheels.

Storing

Divide between 4 airtight containers. Place in the fridge and consume within 3-4 days.

To freeze, transfer to Ziploc bags and freeze up to 3 months. Defrost in the microwave for a couple of minutes to enjoy.

Nutritional Fact per Serving:

Calories: 349; Fat: 22.5g; Net Carbs: 2.2g; Protein: 33g

CAULIFLOWER BEEF CURRY

Total Time: 26 minutes | **Serves:** 4

Ingredients

2 tbsp olive oil
1 ½ pounds ground beef
1 tbsp ginger-garlic paste
½ tsp cumin
¼ tsp allspice
6 oz canned whole tomatoes
1 head cauliflower, cut into florets
Salt and chili pepper to taste

Directions

Cook the beef in hot oil over medium heat for 5 minutes while breaking any lumps. Stir in cumin, allspice, salt, and chili pepper.

Stir in the tomatoes and cauliflower, and cook covered for 6 minutes.

Add a ¼ cup of water and bring to a boil over medium heat for 10 minutes or until the water has reduced by half. Adjust the taste with salt.

Storing

When cooled, divide between 4 airtight containers. Place in the fridge. Use for up to 3 days.

To freeze, transfer to Ziploc bags and freeze up to 3 months. Defrost in the microwave for a few minutes to enjoy.

Nutritional Fact per Serving:

Calories: 518; Fat: 34.6g; Net Carbs: 3g; Protein: 44.6g

STEAK FAJITAS

Total Time: 35 minutes | **Serves:** 4

Ingredients

2 lb sirloin steak, cut into strips
2 tbsp Cajun seasoning
4 oz guacamole
Salt to taste
2 tbsp olive oil
2 shallots, sliced
1 red bell pepper, sliced
8 low carb tortillas

Directions

Preheat grill to 425°F. Rub the steaks all over with Cajun seasoning and place in the fridge for 1 hour.

Grill steaks for 6 minutes on each side, flipping once until lightly browned. Remove from heat and wrap in foil, to let sit for 10 minutes.

Heat the olive oil in a skillet over medium heat and sauté the shallots and bell pepper for 5 minutes or until soft. Share the steaks on the tortillas.

Top with the sauteéd veggies and guacamole.

Storing

When cooled, put the fajitas in individually wrapped aluminium foil and store for up to 3 days in the fridge.

To freeze, transfer to Ziploc bags and freeze up to 3 months. Defrost in the microwave for a few minutes.

Nutritional Fact per Serving:

Calories: 381; Fat: 16.7g; Net Carbs: 5g; Protein: 47g

ROSEMARY CREAMY BEEF

Total Time: 25 minutes | **Serves:** 4

Ingredients

1 tbsp olive oil
3 tbsp butter
2 tbsp rosemary, chopped
1 tbsp garlic powder
4 beef steaks
Salt and black pepper, to taste
1 red onion, chopped
½ cup half-and-half
½ cup beef stock
1 tbsp mustard
2 tsp lemon juice
A sprig of sage
A sprig of thyme

Directions

Rub the olive oil, garlic powder, and chopped rosemary all over the steaks slices and season with salt and black pepper. Using a bowl, combine 1 tbsp of oil black with pepper, garlic, rosemary, and salt.

Heat the butter in a pan over medium heat, place in the beef steaks, and cook for 6 minutes, flipping once halfway through; set aside. In the same pan, add in the red onion, and cook for 3 minutes; stir in the beef stock, thyme sprig, half-and-half, mustard, and sage sprig, and cook for 8 minutes.

Stir in lemon juice, black pepper, and salt. Get rid of the sage and thyme sprigs, and remove from heat.

Storing

Divide the steaks between 4 airtight containers and pour over the sauce, put in the fridge. Best if consumed within 3 days.

To freeze, transfer to Ziploc bags and freeze up to 3 months. Defrost in the microwave and microwave for a couple of minutes to enjoy.

Nutritional Fact per Serving:

Calories: 481; Fat: 25.5g; Net Carbs: 7.8g; Protein: 51.7g

RUSTIC LAMB STEW WITH ROOT VEGGIES

Total Time: 1 hour 45 minutes | **Serves:** 4

Ingredients

2 tbsp olive oil
1 pound lamb chops
1 garlic clove, minced
1 parsnip, chopped
1 onion, chopped
1 celery stalk, chopped
Salt and black pepper, to taste
2 cups vegetable stock
2 carrots, chopped
½ tbsp fresh rosemary, chopped
1 tbsp sweet paprika
1 leek, chopped
1 tbsp tomato paste
½ fennel bulb, chopped

Directions

Warm olive oil in a pot over medium heat and cook celery, onion, leek, and garlic for 5 minutes.

Stir in the lamb chops, and cook for 4 minutes. Add in the sweet paprika, carrots, parsnip, fennel, vegetable stock, tomato paste, and leave to simmer for 1 hour. If it is necessary, add a splash of water. Taste and adjust the seasoning, sprinkle with rosemary, and let cool at room temperature.

Storing

Divide the kale between 4 airtight containers. Place in the fridge and consume within 3-4 days.

To freeze, transfer to Ziploc bags and freeze up to 3 months. Defrost in the microwave for a few minutes to enjoy.

Nutritional Fact per Serving:

Calories: 472; Fat: 37.5g; Net Carbs: 6.3g; Protein: 20.5g

MINTY LAMB WITH BUTTER SAUCE

Total Time: 25 minutes + cooling time | **Serves:** 4

Ingredients

1 ¼ pounds rack of lamb
Salt to cure
3 cloves garlic, minced
3 oz butter, melted

3 oz red wine
A handful of fresh mint, chopped
Water for soaking

Butter Sauce

1 cup vegetable broth
2 tbsp olive oil
1 zucchini, chopped

2 cloves garlic, minced
2 oz butter
Salt and white pepper to taste

Directions

Put the lamb in a large bowl and cover with water to soak for 30 minutes. Let the lamb sit on a rack to drain completely and rinse it afterward. Place in a bowl.

Mix the melted butter with red wine, salt, and 3 garlic cloves, and brush the mixture all over the lamb. Drop the chopped mint on it, cover the bowl with plastic wrap, and place in the refrigerator to marinate.

On the next day, preheat the grill to 435°F and cook the lamb for 6 minutes on both sides. Remove and let rest for 4 minutes.

Heat the olive oil in a frying pan and sauté 2 garlic cloves and zucchini, for 5 minutes. Pour in the vegetable broth and continue cooking the ingredients until the liquid reduces by half, about 10 minutes. Add the 2 oz of butter, salt and pepper. Stir to melt the butter and turn the heat off. Puree the ingredients in a food processor until very smooth and strain the sauce through a fine mesh into a bowl. Slice the lamb.

Storing

When cooled, divide the lamb slices between 4 airtight containers and top each one with the sauce. Place in the fridge. You can use them for up to 3 days.

To freeze, transfer to Ziploc bags and freeze up to 3 months. Defrost in the microwave and microwave for a couple of minutes to enjoy.

Nutritional Fact per Serving:

Calories: 553; Fat: 47.8g; Carbs 2.3g; Protein: 30.2g

Seafood Recipes

CHEESY BAKED TROUT WITH ZUCCHINI

Total Time: 40 minutes | **Serves:** 4

Ingredients

4 deboned trout fillets
2 zucchinis, sliced
1 tbsp butter, melted
Salt and black pepper to taste
1 cup Greek yogurt
¼ cup cheddar cheese, grated
Grated Parmesan cheese for topping

Directions

Preheat oven to 390°F and brush the fish and zucchini slices with melted butter. Season with salt and black pepper to taste, and spread in a greased baking dish.

Mix the Greek yogurt with cheddar cheese, in a bowl. Pour and smear the mixture on the fish, and sprinkle with some Parmesan cheese.

Bake for 25 to 30 minutes until golden brown on top.

Storing

When cooled, divide between 4 airtight containers. Refrigerate for up to 3 days.

To freeze, transfer to Ziploc bags and freeze up to 3 months.

Nutritional Fact per Serving:

Calories: 362; Fat: 23.2g; Net Carbs: 5.8g; Protein: 25.6g

SPEEDY FISH TACOS

Total Time: 20 minutes | **Serves:** 4

Ingredients

1 tbsp olive oil
1 red chili pepper, minced
1 tsp coriander seeds
4 cod fillets, roughly chopped
1 tsp smoked paprika
4 low carb tortillas
Salt and black pepper to taste
1 lemon, juiced

Directions

Season the fish with salt, black pepper and paprika.

Heat the olive oil in a skillet over medium heat. Add cod and chili pepper and stir-fry for about 6 minutes.

Pour in the lemon juice and cook for another 2 minutes.

Divide the fish between the tortillas.

Storing

Divide between 4 airtight containers. Place in the fridge and consume within 3 days.

To freeze, transfer to Ziploc bags and freeze up to 3 months. Defrost in the microwave and garnish with slaw and mayo to serve.

Nutritional Fact per Serving:

Calories: 447; Fat: 21g; Net Carbs: 4.3g; Protein: 24.3g

ASIAN-STYLE STEAMED MUSSELS

Total Time: 25 minutes | **Serves:** 6

Ingredients

5 tbsp sesame oil
1 onion, chopped
3 lb mussels, cleaned
2 garlic cloves, minced
12 oz coconut milk
16 oz white wine
1 lime, juiced
2 tsp red curry powder
A handful of cilantro, chopped

Directions

Warm the sesame oil in a saucepan over medium heat and cook onion and garlic cloves for 3 minutes. Pour in the wine, coconut milk, and red curry powder, and cook for 5 minutes. Add the mussels, turn off the heat, cover the saucepan, and steam the mussels until their shells are opened, about 5-6 minutes.

Discard any closed mussels. Sprinkle with cilantro.

Storing

When cooled, divide between 4 airtight containers. Place in the fridge and consume within 2-3 days.

To freeze, transfer to Ziploc bags and freeze up to 3 months. Defrost in the microwave for a few minutes.

Nutritional Fact per Serving:

Calories: 323; Fat: 16.6g; Net Carbs: 5.4g; Protein: 28.2g

EASY COCONUT COCKTAIL CRAB BALLS

Total Time: 15 minutes | **Serves:** 4

Ingredients

1 lime, juiced
2 tbsp coconut oil
8 oz lump crab meat
2 tsp wasabi sauce
1 egg, beaten
Salt and black pepper to taste
1 tbsp coconut flour

Directions

Mix together the crab meat, wasabi sauce, lime juice, and egg in a bowl. Season with salt and black pepper. Make balls out of the mixture.

Fry in melted coconut oil over medium heat for 5-6 minutes in total; let cool.

Storing

Divide between 4 airtight containers. Place in the fridge and consume within 3 days.

Nutritional Fact per Serving:

Calories: 277; Fat: 10.9g; Net Carbs: 5.1g; Protein: 24.2g

CURRIED HOMEMADE SHRIMP

Total Time: 25 minutes | **Serves:** 4

Ingredients

2 tbsp Parmesan cheese, grated
1 egg, beaten
½ tsp curry powder
2 tsp coconut flour
1 pound shrimp, shelled
3 tbsp coconut oil
2 tbsp curry leaves
2 tbsp butter
1 onion, chopped
½ cup coconut cream
2 tbsp mozzarella cheese, shredded

Directions

In a bowl, combine all dry ingredients for the batter. Melt the coconut oil in a skillet over medium heat. Dip the shrimp in the egg first, and then coat with the dry mixture. Fry until golden and crispy.

In another skillet, melt the butter, and sauté the onion for 3 minutes. Add curry leaves, cook for 30 seconds and stir in the coconut cream and mozzarella cheese, until thickened. Add the shrimp and coat well.

Storing

Divide the kale between 4 airtight containers. Place in the fridge and consume within 3-4 days.

To freeze, transfer to Ziploc bags and freeze up to 3 months. Defrost in the microwave for a few minutes to enjoy.

Nutritional Fact per Serving:

Calories: 422; Fat: 32.2g; Net Carbs: 4.8g; Protein: 29g

PARTY SMOKED SALMON BALLS

Total Time: 30 minutes | **Serves:** 6

Ingredients

1 parsnip, cooked and mashed
Salt and chili pepper to taste
4 tbsp olive oil
12 oz sliced smoked salmon, finely chopped
3 eggs, beaten
2 tbsp pesto sauce
1 tbsp pork rinds, crushed

Directions

In a bowl, add the salmon, eggs, pesto sauce, pork rinds, salt, and chili pepper. With your hands, mix and make 6 compact balls.

Heat olive oil in a skillet over medium heat and fry the balls for 3 minutes on each side until golden brown. Remove to a wire rack to cool.

Storing

Divide between 6 airtight containers in the fridge. Best if consumed within 3 days.

To freeze, transfer to Ziploc bags and freeze up to 3 months. Defrost in the microwave for a couple of minutes to enjoy.

Nutritional Fact per Serving:

Calories: 254; Fat: 18g; Net Carbs: 4.3g; Protein: 17g

FISH FRITTERS

Total Time: 40 minutes + cooling time | **Serves:** 4

Ingredients

1 pound cod fillets, thinly sliced
¼ cup mayonnaise
¼ cup almond flour
2 eggs
Salt and black pepper to taste
1 cup Swiss cheese, grated
1 tbsp chopped dill
3 tbsp olive oil

Directions

Mix the fish, mayonnaise, almond flour, eggs, salt, black pepper, Swiss cheese, and dill, in a bowl. Cover the bowl with plastic wrap and refrigerate for 2 hours.

Warm olive oil in a skillet over medium heat. Fetch 2 tablespoons of fish mixture into the skillet, use the back of a spatula to flatten the top.

Cook for 4 minutes, flip, and fry for 4 more. Remove onto a wire rack and repeat the cooking process until the fish batter is finished, adding more oil as needed.

Storing

When cooled, divide between 4 airtight containers and refrigerate for up to 7 days.

To freeze, transfer to Ziploc bags and freeze up to 3 months. Defrost in the microwave for a couple of minutes.

Nutritional Fact per Serving:

Calories: 633; Fat: 46.9g; Net Carbs: 7g; Protein: 39g

SPICED ROASTED BROCCOLI & CAULIFLOWER STEAKS

Total Time: 30 minutes | **Serves:** 6

Ingredients

1 head broccoli, cut into 1-inch slices
1 head cauliflower, cut into 1-inch slices
2 tbsp olive oil
Salt and chili pepper to taste
1 tsp ground coriander

Directions

Preheat oven to 400°F and line a baking sheet with foil. Brush the broccoli and cauliflower steaks with olive oil and season with chili pepper, coriander, and salt.

Spread on a greased baking sheet in one layer.

Roast in the oven for 10 minutes until tender and lightly browned.

Storing

When cooled, divide between 4 airtight containers and refrigerate for up to 7 days.

To freeze, transfer to Ziploc bags and freeze up to 3 months. Defrost in the microwave for a couple of minutes.

Nutritional Fact per Serving:

Calories: 62; Fat: 4.9g; Net Carbs: 1.4g; Protein: 2.4g

CHICKEN BAKE WITH ONION & PARSNIP

Total Time: 30 minutes | **Serves:** 6

Ingredients

3 parsnips, sliced
1 onion, sliced
4 garlic cloves, crushed
2 tbsp olive oil
2 lb chicken boneless and skinless breasts
½ cup chicken broth
¼ cup white wine
Salt and black pepper to taste

Directions

Preheat oven to 360°F.

Warm the oil in a skillet over medium heat and brown the chicken for a couple of minutes, and transfer them to a baking dish.

Arrange the vegetables around the chicken, add in the white wine and chicken broth and season with salt and black pepper.

Bake in the oven for 23 minutes, stirring the veggie once. Let cool completely.

Storing

When cooled, divide between 4 airtight containers and refrigerate for up to 7 days.

To freeze, transfer to Ziploc bags and freeze up to 3 months. Defrost in the microwave for a couple of minutes.

Nutritional Fact per Serving:

Calories: 278; Fat: 8.7g; Net Carbs: 5.1g; Protein: 35g

MELT-IN-THE-MIDDLE CHICKEN MEATBALLS

Total Time: 20 minutes | **Serves:** 4

Ingredients

2 tbsp olive oil
1 large egg
1 pound ground chicken
1 cup celery, chopped
2 tbsp pork rinds, crushed
2 garlic cloves, minced
2 shallots, chopped
1 tbsp dried oregano
2 tbsp fresh parsley, chopped
Salt and black pepper, to taste
1 cup pecorino cheese, grated

Directions

Put the ground chicken, egg, shallots, garlic, celery, oregano, parsley, black pepper, and salt in a bowl and mix to combine. Form meatballs from the mixture.

Lay the pork rinds on a large plate and roll the meatballs in them. Fry the meatballs in warm olive oil over medium heat on all sides until lightly golden, about 5-6 minutes and transfer to a baking dish.

Scatter the grated cheese over and bake for 5 minutes, until the cheese melts.

Storing

Divide between 4 airtight containers or Ziploc bags and place in the fridge. Use them for up to 3 days.

To freeze, transfer to Ziploc bags and freeze up to 3 months. Defrost in the microwave for a few minutes.

Nutritional Fact per Serving:

Calories: 466; Fat: 35.3g; Net Carbs: 2.7g; Protein: 32.4g

GRUYERE & HAM WAFFLE SANDWICHES

Total Time: 20 minutes | **Serves:** 4

Ingredients

4 tbsp butter, softened
4 slices smoked ham, chopped
½ cup Gruyère cheese, grated
6 eggs
½ tsp baking powder
Salt to taste
½ tsp dried thyme
4 tomato slices

Directions

In a bowl, mix eggs, baking powder, thyme, butter and salt.

Set a waffle iron over medium heat, add in ¼ cup of the batter and cook for 6 minutes until golden. Do the same with the remaining batter until you have 8 thin waffles.

To assemble, lay a tomato slice on top of one waffle, followed by a ham slice, then top with ¼ of the grated cheese.

Cover with another waffle, place the sandwich in the waffle iron and cook until the cheese melts. Do the same with all remaining ingredients, until you have obtained 4 sandwiches.

Storing

When cooled, divide the sandwiches between 4 airtight containers or Ziploc bags and place in the fridge. You can use them for up to 3 days.

To freeze, transfer to Ziploc bags and freeze up to 3 months. Defrost in the microwave and microwave for a couple of minutes to enjoy.

Nutritional Fact per Serving:

Calories: 276; Fat: 22g; Net Carbs: 3.1g; Protein: 16g

NO BAKE CHEESY WALNUT BALLS

Total Time: 15 minutes | **Serves:** 4

Ingredients

1 cup ground walnuts
1 ½ cups feta cheese, crumbled
½ cream cheese, at room temperature
2 tbsp butter, softened
1 habanero pepper, seeded and chopped
¼ tsp parsley flakes
½ tsp hot paprika

Directions

In a bowl, mix all ingredients, except for the walnuts, to combine. Cover with foil and refrigerate for 30 minutes to firm up. Remove from the fridge and form balls from the mixture.

Place the ground walnuts in a plate and roll the balls to coat on all sides.

Storing

When cooled, divide between airtight containers or Ziploc bags and place in the fridge. You can use them for up to 3 days.

Nutritional Fact per Serving:

Calories: 398; Fat: 37g; Net Carbs 5.4g; Protein: 12.4g

SMOKED BACON & POACHED EGG CUPS

Total Time: 20 minutes | **Serves:** 6

Ingredients

4 oz smoked bacon, sliced
6 eggs
2 tbsp chives, chopped
½ cup mozzarella cheese, shredded
4 tbsp sour cream
Salt and black pepper, to taste

Directions

Fry the bacon slices in a pan over medium heat for 4 minutes on both sides.

With the bacon fat, grease 6 ramekins, then line 2 bacon slices on the inside of each cup. Share the sour cream, mozzarella cheese, and crack an egg in each cup. Sprinkle with salt, black pepper and chives.

Bake for 15 minutes in a preheated oven at 400°F, until the eggs are set. Cool before storing.

Storing

Wrap the ramekins with plastic wrap and place in the fridge for up to 7 days.

To freeze, wrap with aluminium foil and freeze for up to 1 month. Defrost in the microwave uncovered for a couple of minutes.

Nutritional Fact per Serving:

Calories: 149; Fat: 10.6g; Net Carbs: 2.4g; Protein: 10.9g

CAULIFLOWER POPCORN WITH WALNUTS & PARSLEY

Total Time: 30 minutes | **Serves:** 4

Ingredients

1 tbsp olive oil
1 head cauliflower, broken into florets
1 cup walnuts, halved
¼ cup Parmesan cheese, grated
1 tsp garlic, smashed
1 tsp turmeric
1 tsp fresh parsley, chopped
1 tsp chili pepper powder
Salt to taste

Directions

Preheat oven to 390°F.

Coat the florets with olive oil, salt, chili pepper powder, garlic, and turmeric.

Pour in a baking dish and add in walnuts and parsley.

Bake in the oven for 25 minutes until crisp. Sprinkle with Parmesan cheese and bake for another 2-3 minutes until the cheese melts.

Storing

When cooled, divide between 4 airtight containers or Ziploc bags and place in the fridge. You can use them for up to 3 days.

To freeze, transfer to Ziploc bags and freeze up to 3 months. Defrost in the microwave and microwave for a couple of minutes to enjoy.

Nutritional Fact per Serving:

Calories: 211; Fat: 18.4g; Net Carbs: 5.7g; Protein: 6.4g

NO-BAKE & EGG BALLS

Total Time: 35 minutes | **Serves:** 6

Ingredients

3 tbsp mayonnaise
2 eggs, cooked and chopped
½ cup butter, softened
8 black olives, pitted and chopped
Salt and crushed red pepper flakes, to taste
1 oz salami, chopped
2 tbsp flax seeds

Directions

Throw the eggs, olives, red pepper flakes, mayonnaise, butter, and salt in a food processor, and blitz until everything is combined. Stir in the chopped salami. Refrigerate for 20 minutes.

Make balls from the mixture. Pour the flax seeds on a large plate; roll the balls through to coat.

Storing

Place the balls in an airtight container and keep in the refrigerator for 4 days.

To freeze, transfer to Ziploc bags and freeze up to 3 months. Defrost in the microwave and microwave for a couple of minutes to enjoy.

Nutritional Fact per Serving:

Calories: 233; Fat: 23.6g; Net Carbs: 1.3g; Protein: 4.4g

Vegan & Vegetarian Recipes

VEGAN BBQ TOFU KABOBS WITH GREEN DIP

Total Time: 20 minutes | **Serves:** 4

Ingredients

½ tbsp BBQ sauce, sugar-free
1 lb extra firm tofu, pressed and cubed
1 tsp salt
1 tbsp vegan butter, melted

Dip

2/3 cup canola oil
5 tbsp fresh cilantro, chopped
3 tbsp fresh basil, chopped
2 garlic cloves
Juice of ½ a lime
4 tbsp capers
Salt and black pepper to taste

Directions

To make the dip, in a blender, add the cilantro, basil, garlic, lemon juice, capers, canola oil, salt and black pepper. Process until smooth, about 1 to 2 minutes. Pour the mixture into a beaker and set aside.

Thread the tofu cubes on wooden skewers to fit into your grill pan. Season with salt and brush with the BBQ sauce. Melt the vegan butter in a grill pan and cook the tofu until browned on both sides. Let cool.

Storing

Place the dip and kabobs into separate containers. Place in the fridge. You can use them for up to 3 days.

To freeze, transfer to Ziploc bags and freeze up to 3 months. Defrost in the microwave for a couple of minutes.

Nutritional Fact per Serving:

Calories: 471; Fat: 47g; Net Carbs: 3.8g; Protein: 11.9g

CHARRED ASPARAGUS WITH CREAMY SAUCE

Total Time: 12 minutes | **Serves:** 4

Ingredients

½ cup coconut cream
Salt and powdered chili pepper to taste
4 tbsp flax seed powder + ½ cup water
¼ cup butter, melted
⅓ cup cashew cheese, grated

Asparagus

1 tbsp olive oil
½ lb asparagus, hard stalks removed
Salt and black pepper
3 oz butter
Juice of ½ a lemon

Directions

Heat the olive oil in a saucepan and roast the asparagus until lightly charred. Season with salt and black pepper, turn the heat off and set aside.

Melt the butter in a frying pan until nutty and golden brown. Stir in the lemon juice and pour the mixture over the asparagus.

In a safe microwave bowl, mix the flax seed powder with water and set aside to thicken for 5 minutes.

Warm the flax egg in the microwave for 1 to 2 minutes, then, pour into a blender. Add the butter, cashew cheese, coconut cream, salt,and chili pepper. Puree the ingredients until well combined and smooth.

Storing

Place the sauce and asparagus in separate containers. Refrigerate for up to 3 days.

To freeze, transfer to Ziploc bags and freeze up to 3 months. Defrost in the microwave for a couple of minutes.

Nutritional Fact per Serving:

Calories: 442; Fat: 45g; Net Carbs: 5.4g; Protein: 5.9g

EGGPLANT & GOAT CHEESE PIZZA

Total Time: 45 minutes | **Serves:** 4

Ingredients

4 tbsp olive oil
2 eggplants, sliced lengthwise
1 cup tomato sauce
2 garlic cloves, minced
1 red onion, sliced
12 oz goat cheese, crumbled
Salt and black pepper to taste
½ tsp cinnamon powder
1 cup mozzarella cheese, shredded
2 tbsp oregano, chopped

Directions

Line a baking sheet with parchment paper. Lay the eggplant slices in a baking dish and drizzle with some olive oil. Bake in the oven until lightly browned, for about 20 minutes at 390°F.

Heat the remaining olive oil in a skillet and sauté the garlic and onion until fragrant and soft, for about 3 minutes.

Stir in the goat cheese, tomato sauce and season with salt and black pepper. Simmer for 10 minutes.

Remove the eggplant from the oven and spread the cheese sauce on top. Sprinkle with the mozzarella cheese and oregano. Bake further for 10 minutes or until the cheese has melted. Let cool and slice.

Storing

When cooled, divide between 4 airtight containers or Ziploc bags and place in the fridge. You can use them for up to 3 days.

To freeze, transfer to Ziploc bags and freeze up to 3 months. Defrost in the microwave and microwave for a couple of minutes to enjoy.

Nutritional Fact per Serving:

Calories: 557; Fat: 44.5g; Net Carbs: 8.3g; Protein: 33.7g

ONE-POT SPICY BRUSSEL SPROUTS WITH CARROTS

Total Time: 15 minutes | **Serves:** 4

Ingredients

1 pound Brussels sprouts
¼ cup olive oil
4 green onions, chopped
1 carrot, grated
Salt and black pepper to taste
Hot chili sauce

Directions

Sauté green onions in warm olive oil over medium heat for 2 minutes, to slightly soften. Stir in the salt and black pepper; transfer to a plate after. Trim the Brussel sprouts and cut in halves. Leave the small ones as wholes.

Pour the Brussel sprouts with and carrot into the same saucepan and stir-fry until softened but al dente.

Season with salt and black pepper, stir in the onions, and heat for a few seconds. Top with the hot chili sauce.

Storing

When cooled, divide between 4 airtight containers or Ziploc bags and place in the fridge. You can use them for up to 3 days.

To freeze, transfer to Ziploc bags and freeze up to 3 months. Defrost in the microwave and microwave for a couple of minutes to enjoy.

Nutritional Fact per Serving:

Calories: 198; Fat: 14.2g; Net Carbs: 6.5g; Protein: 4.9g

TOMATO & MOZZARELLA CAPRESE BAKE

Total Time: 25 minutes | **Serves:** 4

Ingredients

4 tbsp olive oil
4 tomatoes, sliced
1 cup fresh mozzarella cheese, sliced
2 tbsp basil pesto
1 cup mayonnaise
2 oz parmesan cheese
Salt and black pepper

Directions

In a baking dish, arrange the tomatoes and mozzarella slices. In a bowl, mix the basil pesto, mayonnaise, one-ounce parmesan cheese, salt and black pepper, and mix to combine.

Spread this mixture over tomatoes and mozzarella, and top with the remaining parmesan cheese.

Bake for 20 minutes at 360°F or until the top is golden brown. Remove, allow cooling and slice.

Storing

When cooled, divide between 4 airtight containers or Ziploc bags and place in the fridge for up to 3 days.

To freeze, transfer to Ziploc bags and freeze up to 3 months. Defrost in the microwave for a few minutes.

Nutritional Fact per Serving:

Calories: 420; Fat: 36.6g; Net Carbs: 4.9g; Protein: 17g

MUSHROOM WHITE PIZZA

Total Time: 35 minutes | **Serves:** 4

Ingredients

2 tbsp flax egg + 6 tbsp water
½ cup mayonnaise
¾ cup almond flour

1 tbsp psyllium husk powder
1 tsp baking soda
½ tsp salt

Topping

¼ cup mushrooms, sliced
1 tbsp oregano
1 tbsp basil pesto
2 tbsp olive oil

Salt and black pepper
½ cup coconut cream
¾ cup parmesan cheese, shredded
6 black olives

Directions

Combine the flax seed powder with water and allow sitting to thicken for 5 minutes. After, whisk in the mayonnaise, almond flour, psyllium husk powder, baking soda and salt. Allow sitting for 5 minutes.

Pour the batter into a greased baking sheet and spread out with a spatula of ½-inch thickness.

Bake in the oven for 10 minutes at 350°F. In a bowl, mix the mushrooms with the pesto, olive oil, salt and black pepper.

Remove the crust from the oven and spread the coconut cream on top. Add the mushroom mixture and parmesan cheese. Bake the pizza further until the cheese melts, for 8 to 10 minutes. When ready, spread the olives on top.

Storing

When cooled, slice and divide between 4 airtight containers or Ziploc bags and refrigerate for up to 3 days.

To freeze, transfer to Ziploc bags and freeze up to 3 months. Warm in the microwave for 2 minutes to enjoy.

Nutritional Fact per Serving:

Calories: 346; Fat: 32.7g; Net Carbs: 5.5g; Protein: 8.5g

VEGAN GARAM MASALA TRAYBAKE

Total Time: 30 minutes | **Serves:** 4

Ingredients

3 tbsp vegan butter
3 cups tempeh slices
1 turnip, sliced
Salt to taste
2 tbsp garam masala
1 cup mushrooms, sliced
1 ¼ cups coconut cream
1 tbsp fresh cilantro, finely chopped

Directions

Place a skillet over medium heat and melt the vegan butter. Fry the tempeh until browned on both sides, about 4 minutes; season with salt. Stir half of the garam masala into the tempeh until evenly mixed and turn the heat off.

Transfer the tempeh with the spice into a baking dish and set aside.

In a bowl, mix the mushrooms, turnip, coconut cream, cilantro, and remaining garam masala. Pour the mixture over the tempeh and bake in the oven for 20 minutes at 400°F or until golden brown on top. Garnish with cilantro.

Storing

When cooled, divide between 4 airtight containers or Ziploc bags and place in the fridge. Consume within 3 days.

To freeze, put in Ziploc bags and freeze up to 3 months. Defrost in the microwave for a few minutes.

Nutritional Fact per Serving:

Calories: 591; Fat: 48.4g; Net Carbs: 9.4g; Protein: 28.2g

MASCARPONE AND KALE ASIAN CASSEROLE

Total Time: 30 minutes | **Serves:** 4

Ingredients

2 cups tofu, grilled and cubed
1 cup smoked seitan, chopped
1 cup mascarpone cheese
1 tbsp mustard powder
1 tbsp plain vinegar
1 ¼ cups cheddar cheese, shredded
Salt and black pepper
½ cup kale, chopped
2 tbsp olive oil

Directions

Mix the mascarpone cheese, mustard powder, plain vinegar, kale, and cheddar cheese in a greased baking dish. Top with the tofu, seitan, and season with salt and black pepper.

Bake in the oven until the casserole is golden brown on top, for about 15 to 20 minutes, at 400°F.

Storing

When cooled, divide between 4 airtight containers or Ziploc bags and place in the fridge. You can use them for up to 3 days.

To freeze, transfer to Ziploc bags and freeze up to 3 months. Defrost in the microwave and microwave for a couple of minutes to enjoy.

Nutritional Fact per Serving:

Calories: 612; Fat: 51g; Net Carbs: 9.1g; Protein: 30.5g

CAULIFLOWER & BROCCOLI GRATIN WITH SEITAN

Total Time: 40 minutes | **Serves:** 4

Ingredients

4 tbsp avocado oil
2 shallots, chopped
2 cups broccoli florets
1 cup cauliflower florets
2 cups seitan, crumbled
1 cup heavy cream
2 tbsp mustard powder
5 oz pecorino cheese, shredded
4 tbsp fresh rosemary, chopped
Salt and black pepper to taste

Directions

Put half of the avocado oil in a pot, and set over medium heat to melt. Add the shallots, broccoli, and cauliflower and cook until the vegetables have softened, for about 6 minutes. Transfer the vegetables to a baking dish.

Warm the remaining avocado oil in a skillet over medium heat, and cook the seitan until browned. Mix the heavy cream and mustard powder in a bowl. Then, pour the mixture over the vegetables.

Scatter the seitan and pecorino cheese on top and sprinkle with rosemary, salt and pepper. Bake for 15 minutes at 400 F. Remove and let cool before storing.

Storing

When cooled, divide between 4 airtight containers or Ziploc bags and place in the fridge. You can use them for up to 3 days.

To freeze, transfer to Ziploc bags and freeze up to 3 months. Defrost in the microwave and microwave for a couple of minutes to enjoy.

Nutritional Fact per Serving:

Calories: 753; Fat: 37g; Net Carbs: 12g; Protein: 86g

BAKED CREAMY BRUSSELS SPROUTS

Total Time: 25 minutes | **Serves:** 4

Ingredients

3 tbsp ghee
1 cup tempeh, cubed
1 pound Brussels sprouts, halved
5 garlic cloves, minced
1 ¼ cups crème fraîche
1 ⅓ cups white cheddar cheese, shredded
¼ cup Gruyère cheese, shredded
Salt and black pepper to taste

Directions

Melt the ghee in a large skillet over medium heat and fry the tempeh cubes until browned on both sides, for about 6 minutes. Remove to a plate and set aside.

Pour the Brussels sprouts and garlic into the skillet and sauté until nice color forms and fragrant. Stir in crème fraîche and simmer for 4 minutes. Add tempeh cubes and mix well.

Pour the sautéed ingredients into a baking dish, sprinkle with cheddar cheese and Gruyère cheese. Bake for 10 minutes at 400 F or until golden brown on top.

Storing

When cooled, divide between 4 airtight containers or Ziploc bags. Refrigerate for up to 3 days.

To freeze, transfer to Ziploc bags and freeze up to 3 months. Defrost in the microwave for a few minutes to enjoy.

Nutritional Fact per Serving:

Calories: 563; Fat: 44.5g; Net Carbs: 8.7g; Protein: 25.2g

EASY CHEESY GREEN PIZZA

Total Time: 40 minutes | **Serves:** 4

Ingredients

2 tbsp flax seed powder + 6 tbsp water
1 cup broccoli, grated
1 red bell pepper, sliced
¾ cup + ½ cup parmesan cheese, shredded
½ tsp salt
2 tbsp marinara sauce
¼ cup mozzarella cheese
¼ cup canned artichokes, cut into wedges
1 garlic clove, thinly sliced
1 tbsp dried oregano

Directions

In a medium bowl, mix the flax seed powder and water and allow thickening for 5 minutes. When the flax egg is ready, add the broccoli, ¾ cup of parmesan cheese, salt, and stir to combine well.

Pour the mixture into a baking sheet and spread out with a spatula. Bake until the crust is lightly browned, for about 20 minutes at 350°F.

Remove from the oven and spread the marinara sauce on top, sprinkle with the remaining parmesan cheese, mozzarella cheese, artichokes, red bell pepper slices, and sliced garlic.

Spread the oregano on top. Bake the pizza further for 5 to 10 minutes at 420 F or until the cheese has melted and lightly browned. Slice the pizza when cooled.

Storing

When cooled, divide between 4 airtight containers or Ziploc bags and place in the fridge. You can use them for up to 3 days.

To freeze, transfer to Ziploc bags and freeze up to 3 months. Defrost in the microwave and microwave for a couple of minutes to enjoy.

Nutritional Fact per Serving:

Calories: 108; Fat: 5.4g; Net Carbs: 4.8g; Protein: 9.2g

Desserts

ALMOND ICE CREAM

Total Time: 3 hours 40 minutes | **Serves:** 4

Ingredients

2 cups heavy cream
1 tbsp xylitol
½ cup smooth almond butter
1 tbsp olive oil
1 tbsp vanilla extract
½ tsp salt
2 egg yolks
½ cup swerve sweetener confectioners
½ cup almonds, chopped

Directions

Warm the heavy cream with almond butter, olive oil, xylitol, and salt in a small pan over low heat without boiling, for about 3 minutes.

Beat the egg yolks until creamy in color. Stir the eggs into the cream mixture.

Refrigerate the cream mixture for 30 minutes, and stir in swerve sweetener confectioners.

Pour the mixture into ice cream machine and churn it according to the manufacturer's instructions. Stir in the almonds and spoon the mixture into loaf pan.

Place in the fridge at least for two hours before consuming.

Storing

You can keep the ice cream in the freezer for up to 2 months.

Nutritional Fact per Serving:

Calories: 552; Fat: 45.4g; Net Carbs: 6.2g; Protein: 9.2g

BLUEBERRY TART

Total Time: 45 minutes | **Serves:** 4

Ingredients

4 eggs
2 tsp coconut oil
2 cups blueberries
1 cup coconut milk
1 cup almond flour
¼ cup sweetener
½ tsp vanilla powder
1 tbsp powdered sweetener
A pinch of salt

Directions

Preheat oven to 350°F. Place all ingredients except coconut oil, berries, and powdered sweetener, in a blender, and blend until smooth. Gently fold in the berries.

Grease a baking dish with the oil. Pour the mixture into the prepared dish and bake for 35 minutes. Sprinkle with powdered sweetener.

Storing

Place the tart in a resealable container and store for up to 7 days at room temperature.

To freeze, place in a freezer-safe container for up to 3 months. Defrost at room temperature.

Nutritional Fact per Serving:

Calories: 355; Fat: 14.5g; Net Carbs: 6.9g; Protein: 11.8g

MATCHA FAT BOMBS

Total Time: 3 min + cooling time | **Serves:** 4

Ingredients

½ cup coconut oil
1 tbsp vanilla extract
½ cup almond butter
4 tbsp matcha powder powder
½ cup xylitol

Directions

Melt butter and coconut oil in a small saucepan over low heat, stirring twice until properly melted and mixed. Mix in matcha powder and xylitol until completely combined.

Pour into muffin moulds and refrigerate for 3 hours to harden.

Storing

Place the fat bombs in a resealable container and store for up to 5 days in the fridge.

To freeze, transfer to Ziploc bags and freeze for up to 3 months.

Nutritional Fact per Serving:

Calories: 436; Fat: 44.6g; Net Carbs: 3.1g; Protein: 6.6g

MASCARPONE ICE BOMBS

Total Time: 2 hrs 10 minutes | **Serves:** 4

Ingredients

2 tbsp butter, melted
1 cup mascarpone cheese, at room temperature
4 tbsp xylitol
2 tbsp coffee
2 tbsp cocoa powder, unsweetened
2 ½ oz dark chocolate, melted

Directions

Blitz mascarpone cheese, xylitol, coffee, and cocoa powder, in a food processor until well mixed. Roll 2 tbsp of the mixture and place on a lined tray.

Mix the melted butter and chocolate, and coat the bombs with it. Freeze for 2 hours.

Storing

Place the fat bombs in a resealable container and store for up to 5 days in the fridge.

To freeze, transfer to Ziploc bags and freeze for up to 3 months.

Nutritional Fact per Serving:

Calories: 286; Fat: 23.7g; Net Carbs: 7.2g; Protein: 10g

PEANUT BUTTER ALMOND COOKIES

Total Time: 25 minutes | **Serves:** 4

Ingredients

½ cup peanut butter, softened
2 cups almond flour
½ tsp baking soda
¾ cup xylitol
A pinch of salt

Coating:

2 tbsp xylitol
1 tsp ground cardamon pods

Directions

Combine peanut butter, almond flour, baking soda, xylitol, and salt in a bowl. Form balls out of the mixture and flatten them with hands.

Combine the cardamon and xylitol. Dip the biscuits in the cardamon mixture and arrange them on a lined cookie sheet. Cook in a preheated oven for 15-20 minutes, until crispy, at 350 F.

Storing

Place the biscuits in a resealable container and store for up to 7 days at room temperature.

To freeze, place in a freezer-safe container for up to 3 months. Defrost at room temperature.

Nutritional Fact per Serving:

Calories: 96; Fat: 6.1g; Net Carbs: 7.4g; Protein: 2.4g

Measurement conversions

Cups to tablespoons	Metric to standard	Fahrenheit to Celsius	Oz to grams
3 tsp = 1 tbsp	5 ml = 1 tsp	300 F = 150 C	1 oz = 28 g
⅛ cup = 2 tbsp	15 ml = 1 tbsp	350 F = 180 C	2 oz = 57 g
¼ cup = 4 tbsp	30 ml = 1 fluid oz	375 F = 190 C	3 oz = 84 g
⅓ cup = 5 tbsp + 1 tsp	240 ml = 1 cup	400 F = 200 C	4 oz = 112 g
½ cup = 8 tbsp	1 liter = 34 fluid oz	425 F = 220 C	5 oz = 142 g
¾ cup = 12 tbsp	1 liter = 4.2 cups	450 F = 230 C	6 oz = 170 g
1 cup = 16 tbsp	1 gram = 0.035 oz		7 oz = 198 g
8 fluid oz = 1 cup	100 grams = 3.5 oz		8 oz = 227 g
1 pint 2 cups = 16 fluid oz	500 grams = 1.10 lb		10 oz = 283 g
1 quart 2 pints = 4 cups			20 oz = 567 g
1 gallon 4 quarts = 16 cups			30 oz = 850 g
			40 oz = 1133 g

Recipe Index

Can't resist buying from a burger stand
dropping into a bakery for something swe
The world doesn't end if you do so once i
while. However, if added up, you may quic
realize you are spending too much money
stuff you could easily do without.

We may argue that's just the way life is or r
but one thing is for sure - it doesn't take m
to make it way better. Planning meals in
organized way for the whole week (or mc
may sound like a signi cant investment but
reality, it saves us a lot of time and money.

How much happier would your family, partr
or friends then be? How much more ti
you would you have for yourself? How m
money would there be left in your pocke
you stopped spending it randomly whene
you have a whim?

If you wonder if a conventional cookbook
offer you so much, the answer is simple -
Not a conventional one. But this Keto I
Meal Prep cookbook - oh YES! This book
culinary response to modern people's nee

ISBN 9781096581956

9 781096 581956